ARTISTS OF THE RIGHT

RESISTING DECADENCE

by

K. R. BOLTON

EDITED BY GREG JOHNSON

Counter-Currents Publishing Ltd.
San Francisco
2012

Cover image: Portrait of Ezra Pound by Wyndham Lewis

Cover design by Kevin I. Slaughter

Published in the United States by
COUNTER-CURRENTS PUBLISHING LTD.
P.O. Box 22638
San Francisco, CA 94122
USA
http://www.counter-currents.com/

Hardcover ISBN: 978-1-935965-13-8
Paperback ISBN: 978-1-935965-14-5
E-book ISBN: 978-1-935965-15-2

Library of Congress Cataloging-in-Publication Data

Bolton, K. R. (Kerry Raymond), 1956-
Artists of the right : resisting decadence / by K. R. Bolton ;
edited with a foreword by Greg Johnson.
p. cm.
Includes bibliographical references and index.
ISBN 978-1-935965-13-8 (hardcover : alk. paper) -- ISBN 978-1-935965-14-5 (pbk. : alk. paper) -- ISBN 978-1-935965-15-2 (ebook)
1. Literature--20th century--History and criticism. 2. Fascism and literature. I. Johnson, Greg, 1971- II. Title.

PN56.F35B65 2012
809'.93358--dc23

2012014610

CONTENTS

FOREWORD

Leftists think that their belief in human equality makes them better than the rest of us. They are particularly wedded to the idea that they are not just the party of humanity but of the intellectual and artistic elites. Thus it is a profound embarrassment to the Left that some of the greatest creative minds of the twentieth century—including leading modernists—were men of the Right, and not just conservatives, but fascists, National Socialists, and fellow travelers.

Kerry Bolton's *Artists of the Right: Resisting Decadence* focuses on ten leading twentieth-century literary figures: D. H. Lawrence, H. P. Lovecraft, Gabriele D'Annunzio, Filippo Marinetti, W. B. Yeats, Knut Hamsun, Ezra Pound, Wyndham Lewis, Henry Williamson, and Roy Campbell.

All ten were immensely accomplished. Yeats and Hamsun both won the Nobel Prize in Literature. Lawrence, Pound, Marinetti, and D'Annunzio were commanding figures of their day. Campbell, Williamson, and Lewis (the last a first-rate painter as well) enjoyed smaller but intensely appreciative audiences, whereas Lovecraft's growing fame is almost entirely posthumous.

As Joseph S. Salemi has remarked, the independence of mind that allowed these artists to break from Left-wing orthodoxy also prevented them from forming a new orthodoxy of the Right. They disagreed on many issues, including religion, economics, and the finer points of political ideology.

Yet to a man, they were united in their rejection of human equality—the common root of capitalism and communism—and their affirmation of a hierarchical model of society. Yet they sought a hierarchical society free of exploitation and invidious distinctions, upholding an organic model of society in which all parts must serve the common good of the whole. Finally, they were united in their rejection of atomistic individualism, although they also affirmed the possibility of creative and heroic individualism.

As Rightists, these artists rejected modern decadence and sought to preserve and restore healthier pre-modern social forms within the context of modernity. As artists, they often explored modern decadence from the inside, even as they upheld a longing for something higher: a form of life characterized by health, beauty, wholeness, and sanctity, based on models from classical Antiquity, the Middle Ages, or the natural world. They also combatted decadence by seeking to release vital creative forces imprisoned by ossified artistic traditions, often giving rise to startling forms of modernism, including Vorticism and Futurism.

With the exception of the chapter on Lovecraft, *Artists of the Right* consists of extensively expanded and reworked essays from Kerry Bolton's earlier book *Thinkers of the Right: Challenging Materialism* (Luton, England: Luton Publications, 2003). A companion volume will cover T. S. Eliot, Yukio Mishima, Rex Fairburn, P. R. Stephensen, Count Potocki of Montalk, and others.

I wish to thank Kerry Bolton for his hard work, patience, and good humor over the long process of bringing this project to birth. I also wish to thank Matthew Peters for his meticulous proofreading, Kevin Slaughter for designing the cover, Michael Polignano for preparing the manuscript for the Library of Congress cataloguing process, and Jonathan Bowden, Leo Yankevich, Dr. Joseph S. Salemi, Charles Krafft, and James J. O'Meara for their blurbs.

Greg Johnson
San Francisco
August 7, 2012

ACKNOWLEDGEMENTS

My acknowledgements and thanks to those who wrote encouraging prepublication appraisals: the late, lamented Jonathan Bowden, Leo Yankevich, Dr. Joseph S. Salemi, Charles Krafft, and James J. O'Meara. Thank you for the encouraging words. To my friend and colleague in Athens, Dr. Dimitris Michalopoulos, for his enthusiastic comments on the 2003 precursor of the book; veteran British nationalist Keith Thompson for the original idea of a book; Dr. Greg Johnson, for suggesting its further development into the present volume, and undertaking the editing; and Matthew Peters for his incomparably meticulous proofreading.

Kerry R. Bolton
Kapiti Coast
New Zealand
September 17, 2012

CHAPTER 1

D. H. LAWRENCE

"My great religion is a belief in the blood."
—D. H. Lawrence[1]

DAVID HERBERT LAWRENCE, 1885–1930, is acknowledged as one of the most influential novelists of the twentieth century. He wrote novels and poetry as acts of polemic and prophecy. For Lawrence saw himself as a prophet and the harbinger of a new dawn as well as a leader-savior who would sacrificially accept the tremendous responsibilities of dictatorial power to free humanity to return to being human. Much of Lawrence's outlook is reminiscent of those of C. G. Jung and Friedrich Nietzsche, but although he was acquainted with the works of both, his philosophy developed independently.

Lawrence was born into a family of colliers in Eastwood, a coal-mining town near Nottingham. His father was a heavy drinker, and his mother was committed to Christianity, thus the house was rife with tension between the parents. At college, he was an agnostic and was determined to become a poet and an author. Having rejected the faith of his mother, Lawrence also rejected the counter-faith of science, democracy, industrialization, and the mechanization of man.

LOVE, POWER, & THE "DARK LORD"

For Lawrence capitalism destroyed the soul and the

---

[1] D. H. Lawrence, letter to Ernest Collings, January 17, 1913, *The Letters of D. H. Lawrence*, vol. 1, ed. James T. Boulton (Cambridge: Cambridge University Press, 1979), p. 503.

mystery of life, as did democracy and equality. He devoted most of his life to finding a new-yet-old religion that would return mystery to life and reconnect humanity to the cosmos.

His religion was animistic and pantheistic, seeing the soul as pervasive, God as nature, and humanity as the way God realizes himself.[2] The relations between all things are based on duality—opposites in tension. This duality is expressed in two ways: love and power. One without the other results in imbalance. Hence, to Lawrence, Christian love is a sentimentality that destroys the natural hierarchy of social relations and the inequality between individuals. This critique of Christianity is reminiscent of Nietzsche, and indeed Lawrence has been described as "Nietzsche's major English disciple."[3]

Love and power are the two "threat vibrations" which hold individuals together and emanate unconsciously from the leadership class.[4] With power, there is trust, fear, and obedience. With love, there is "protection" and "the sense of safety."

Lawrence considers that most leaders have been out of balance with one or the other. That is the message of his novel *Kangaroo.* Here the Englishman Richard Lovat Somers, although attracted to the fascist ideology of "Kangaroo" and his Diggers movement, ultimately rejects it as representing the same type of enervating love as Christianity, the love of the masses, and pursues his own individuality. The question for Somers is that of accepting his own

---

[2] Graham Hough, *The Dark Sun: A Study of D. H. Lawrence* (London: Duckworth, 1956), pp. 223–24.

[3] John Carey, *The Intellectuals and the Masses: Pride and Prejudice Among the Literary Intelligentsia, 1880–1939* (London: Faber & Faber, 1992), p. 75.

[4] Hough, *The Dark Sun*, p. 240.

dark master (Jung's Shadow of the repressed unconscious). Until that returns, no human lordship can be accepted:

> He did not yet submit to the fact which he *half* knew: that before mankind would accept any man for a king, and before Harriet would ever accept him, Richard Lovat, as a lord and master, he, this selfsame Richard who was strong on kingship must open the doors of his soul and let in a dark Lord and Master for himself, the dark god he had sensed outside the door. Let him once truly submit to the dark majesty, break open his doors to this fearful god who is master, and enters us from below, the lower doors; let himself once admit a Master, the unspeakable god: and the rest would happen.[5]

What is required, once the dark lord has returned to men's souls in place of undifferentiated "love," is a hierarchical social order shaped like a pyramid whose apex is a dictator.[6] The dictator would relieve the masses of the burden of democracy. This new social order would be based on the balance of power and love, something of a return to the medieval ideal of protection and obedience.[7]

The ordinary folk would gain a new worth by giving obedience to the leader, who would in turn assume an awesome responsibility and would lead by virtue of his being "circuited" to the cosmos. Through such a redeeming philosopher-king, individuals could reconnect cosmically and assume heroic proportions through obedience to

---

[5] D. H. Lawrence, *Kangaroo* (1923) (London: Heinemann, 1955), ch. 9, "Harriet and Lovat at Sea in Marriage."

[6] D. H. Lawrence, *Selected Literary Criticism* (London: Heinemann, 1955), p. 236.

[7] D. H. Lawrence, *Apocalypse* (London: Secker, 1932), p. 217.

heroes. "Give homage and allegiance to a hero, and you become yourself heroic, it is the law of man."[8]

Heroic Vitalism

Hence, heroic vitalism is central to Lawrence's ideas. His entire political philosophy is antithetical to what he called "the three fanged serpent of Liberty, Equality, Fraternity." Instead, "you must have a government based on good, better, and best."

In 1922 he wrote: "I don't believe either in liberty or democracy. I believe in actual, sacred, inspired authority: divine right of natural kings: I believe in the divine right of natural aristocracy, the right, the sacred duty, to wield undisputed authority."[9] It is mere intellect, soulless and mechanistic, which is at the root of our problems; it restrains the passions and kills the natural.[10]

His essay on *Lady Chatterley's Lover* deals with the social question. It is the mechanistic outlook, arising from pure intellect, devoid of emotion, passion, and all that is implied in the blood (instinct) that has caused the ills of modern society:

> This again is the tragedy of social life today. In the old England, the curious blood connection held the classes together. The squires might be arrogant, violent, bullying, and unjust, yet in some ways they were at one with the people, part of the same blood stream. We feel it in Defoe or Fielding. And then in

---

[8] Lawrence, *Selected Literary Criticism*, p. 105.

[9] Warren Roberts, James T. Boulton, and Elisabeth Mansfield, eds., *The Letters of D. H. Lawrence*, vol. 4, *1921–1924* (Cambridge: Cambridge University Press, 1987), p. 227.

[10] John R. Harrison, *The Reactionaries: A Study of the Anti-Democratic Intelligentisa* (London: Gollancz, 1966), p. 167.

> the mean Jane Austen, it is gone . . . So, in *Lady Chatterley's Lover* we have a man, Sir Clifford, who is purely a personality, having lost entirely all connection with his fellow men and women, except those of usage. All warmth is gone entirely, the hearth is cold, the heart does not humanly exist. He is a pure product of our civilization, but he is the death of the great humanity of the world.[11]

In 1913 Lawrence posited, against this pallid intellectualism, the product of the late phase of a civilization: "My great religion is a belief in the blood, the flesh, as being wiser than the intellect. We can go wrong in our minds. But what our blood feels and believes and says, is always true."[12]

The great cultural figures of our time, including Lawrence, W. B. Yeats, Ezra Pound, and Knut Hamsun, were "Thinkers of the Blood," men of instinct, which has permanence and eternity. Rightly, since the 1930s the term "intellectual" became synonymous with the "Left," but such intellectuals are products of their time and the century before. They are detached from tradition, uprooted, alienated, bereft of instinct and feeling.

The first Thinkers of the Blood, influenced greatly by Nietzsche, championed excellence and nobility and were suspicious if not terrified of the mass leveling resulting from democracy and its offspring communism. In democracy and communism, they saw the destruction of culture understood as the pursuit of the sublime. Their opposite numbers, the intellectuals of the Left, celebrated the rise of mass man in a perverse manner that would, if com-

---

[11] D. H. Lawrence, *A Propos of Lady Chatterley's Lover* (London: Secker and Warburg, 1941), p. 333.

[12] Lawrence, letter of January, 17, 1913, *Letters*, vol. 1, p. 503.

munism were universally triumphant, mean the destruction of their own liberty to create above and beyond the state commissariats.

Lawrence believed that socialistic agitation and unrest would create the climate in which he would be able to gather around him "a choice minority, more fierce and aristocratic in spirit" to take over authority in a fascist-like *coup*, "then I shall come into my own."[13]

Lawrence's rebellion is against that late or winter phase of civilization, which the West has entered as described by Oswald Spengler. It is marked by the rise of the city over the village, of money over blood. Like Spengler, Lawrence's conception of history is cyclic, and his idea of society organic. He wished to break the death grip of late civilization and to revive the organic over the mechanistic.[14]

RELIGION OLD & NEW

Lawrence sought a return to the pagan outlook with its communion with life and the cosmic rhythm. He was drawn to blood mysticism and what he called the dark gods. It was the "Dark God" that embodied all that had been repressed by late civilization and the artificial world of money and industry. His quest took him around the world. Reaching New Mexico in 1922, he observed the rituals of the Pueblo Indians. He then went to Old Mexico where he stayed for several years.

It was in Mexico that he encountered Quetzalcoatl, the Plumed Serpent of the Aztecs. Through a revival of this deity and the reawakening of long-repressed primal urges, Lawrence thought that Europe might be renewed. He

---

[13] Lawrence, Letter to Robert Mountsier, July 17, 1922, *Letters*, vol. 4, p. 277.

[14] Oswald Spengler, *The Decline of the West*, trans. Charles Francis Atkinson, 2 vols. (London: George Allen and Unwin, 1971).

advised the United States to look to the land before the Spaniards and the Pilgrim Fathers and embrace the "black demon of savage America."[15] This "demon" is akin to Jung's concept of the Shadow (and its embodiment in what Jung called the "Devil archetype"). Bringing it to consciousness is required for true wholeness or individuation.

Turn to "the unresolved, the rejected," Lawrence advised the Americans in the periodical *Phoenix*.[16] He regarded his novel *The Plumed Serpent* as his most important. It is the story of a white women who becomes immersed in a social and religious movement of national regeneration among the Mexicans, based on a revival of the worship of Quetzalcoatl.

Through the American Indians Lawrence hoped to see a lesson for Europe. He has one of the leaders of the Quetzalcoatl revival, Don Ramón, say:

> I wish the Teutonic world would once more think in terms of Thor and Wotan and the tree Yggdrasill. And I wish the Druidic world would see, honestly, that in the mistletoe is their mystery, and that they themselves are the Tuatha De Danaan, alive, but submerged. And a new Hermes should come back to the Mediterranean, and a new Ashtaroth to Tunis; and Mithras again to Persia, and Brahma unbroken to India, and the oldest of dragons to China. Then I, Cipriano, I, First Man of Quetzalcoatl, with you, First Man of Huitzilopochtli, and perhaps your wife, First Woman of Itzpapalotl, could we not meet, with sure souls, the other great aristocrats of the world, the

---

[15] D. H. Lawrence, "America, Listen to Your Own," *Phoenix: The Posthumous Papers of D. H. Lawrence* (1936), ed. Edward MacDonald (Harmondsworth: Penguin, 1978), p. 90.

[16] Lawrence, *Phoenix*, p. 90.

> First Man of Wotan and the First Woman of Freya, First Lord of Hermes, and the Lady of Astarte, the Best-Born of Brahma, and the Son of the Greatest Dragon? I tell you, Cipriano, then the earth might rejoice, when the First Lords of the West met the First Lords of South and East, in the Valley of the Soul. Ah, the earth has Valleys of the Soul, that are not cities of commerce and industry. And the mystery is one mystery, but men must see it differently.[17]

Looking about Europe for such a heritage, he found it among the Etruscans and the Druids. Yet although finding his way back to the spirituality that had once been part of Europe, Lawrence does not advocate the mimicking of ancient ways for the present time; nor the adoption of alien spirituality for the European West, as is the fetish among many alienated souls today who look at every culture and heritage except their own. He wishes to return to the substance, to the awe before the mystery of life. "My way is my own, old red father: I can't cluster at the drum anymore," he writes in his essay "Indians and an Englishman."[18] Yet what he found among the Indians was a far-off innermost place at the human core, which he characterizes as the ever present in his description of the way Kate is affected by the ritual she witnesses among the followers of Quetzalcoatl.

In "The Woman Who Rode Away," the wife of a mine owner, tired of her life, leaves to find a remote Indian hill tribe who are said to preserve the rituals of the old gods. She is told that the whites have captured the sun, and she is to be the messenger to tell them to return him. She is

---

[17] D. H. Lawrence, *The Plumed Serpent* (London: Secker, 1926), ch. 17, "Fourth Hymn and the Bishop."

[18] Lawrence, *Phoenix*, p. 99.

sacrificed to the sun. It is a sacrifice of a product of the mechanistic society for a reconnection with the cosmos. For Lawrence the most value is to be had in "the life that arises from the blood."[19]

THE LION, THE UNICORN, & THE CROWN

Lawrence's concept of the dual nature of life, in which there is continual conflict between polarities,[20] is a dialectic that is synthesized. Lawrence uses symbolism to describe this. The lion (the mind, the active, the male) is in eternal strife with the unicorn (the senses, the passive, the female). But if one completely killed the other, it would itself be extinguished, and a vacuum would emerge from the victory.[21] This is so with ideologies, religions, and moralities that stand for the victory of one polarity and the repression of the other. The crown belongs to neither. It stands above both as the symbol of balance.[22] This is something of a Tao for the West, which Jung also sought, and for which the old alchemists quested on an individual basis.[23]

The problems Lawrence brought under consideration have become ever more acute as our late phase of Western civilization draws to a close, dominated by money and the machine. Lawrence, like Yeats, Hamsun, and Henry Williamson, sought a return to the Eternal, by reconnecting to that part of ourselves that has been deeply repressed by the "loathsome spirit of the age."

---

[19] D. H. Lawrence, *The Woman Who Rode Away and Other Stories* (London: Secker, 1928).

[20] Hough, *The Dark Sun*, p. 224.

[21] D. H. Lawrence, "The Crown," *Reflections on the Death of a Porcupine & Other Essays* (Philadelphia: The Centaur Press, 1925).

[22] Hough, *The Dark Sun*, 226.

[23] C. G. Jung, *Alchemical Studies, Collected Works of C. G. Jung*, vol. 13 (Princeton: Princeton University Press, 1938).

CHAPTER 2

H. P. LOVECRAFT

> "We regard the rise of democratic ideas as a sign of cultural old age and decay, and deem it a compliment to such men as Mussolini when they are said to be 'XVth century types.' We are proud to be definitely reactionary, since only by a bold repudiation of the word 'liberal' and the progress illusion can we get the sort of authoritative social and political control which alone produces things which make life worth living."
>
> —H. P. Lovecraft

HOWARD PHILIPS LOVECRAFT, 1890–1937, was a master of looming, irrational, metaphysical horror. But to many of his admirers, the scariest things he wrote were not about Cthulhu, they were about politics. As I hope to show, however, Lovecraft's politics are solidly grounded in reality and reason.

Lovecraft, like many of the literati who turned to Left- or Right-wing politics early in the twentieth century, was concerned with the impact of capitalism and technology on society and culture. The economic reductionism of capitalism was simply mirrored by Marxism, both of them emanations of the same modern materialist *Zeitgeist*.

Beginning in the late nineteenth century, a pervasive discontent with materialism led to a search for an alternative form of society, including alternative foundations for socialism, which occupied Europe's leading socialist minds like Georges Sorel. What emerged early in the twentieth century was variously called "neosocialism" and "planism," the most prominent exponents of which were Marcel Déat in France and Hendrik de Man in Belgium. Neosocialism, in turn, influenced the rise of fascism.[1]

Neosocialists primarily feared that the material abundance and leisure promised by socialism would lead to decadence and banality unless joined to a hierarchical vision of culture and education.

This was, for instance, the focus of Oscar Wilde's "The Soul of Man under Socialism," which envisioned an individualistic socialism that would liberate humanity from economic necessity to pursue self-actualization and higher cultural and spiritual activities, even if these consisted of nothing more than quietly contemplating the cosmos.[2]

Such concerns cannot be dismissed as effete dandyism. They were shared, for instance, by the famous Depression era New Zealand Labour politician John A. Lee, a one-armed hero of the First World War who more than any other individual tried to pressure the 1935 Labour Government into keeping its election pledges on banking and state credit.[3] In Lee's words:

---

[1] Zeev Sternhell, *Neither Left nor Right: Fascist Ideology in France,* trans. David Maisel (Princeton: Princeton University Press, 1986).

[2] Oscar Wilde, "The Soul of Man Under Socialism" (1891), in *The Complete Works of Oscar Wilde,* ed. Merlin Holland (London: HarperCollins, 2003).

[3] After the tour of C. H. Douglas to New Zealand, the banking system and usury were very well understood by the masses of people, and banking reform was a major platform that achieved Labour's victory. As it transpired, they attempted to renege, but Lee succeeded in getting the government to issue 1% Reserve Bank state credit to build the iconic and enduring State Housing project that in one fell swoop reduced unemployment by 75%. Lee soon became a bitter opponent of the opportunism of the Labour politicians. However the state cred-

> Joe Savage . . . sees socialism as piles of goods fairly equitably divided and work equitably divided. I am sure [he] never sees it as the opportunity to play football, get brown on a beach, dance a fox trot, lie on one's back beneath the trees, enjoy the intoxication of verse, the perfume of flowers, the joys of a novel, the thrill of music.[4]

Lee envisioned a form of socialism that was not directed primarily towards "piles of goods and work equitably divided" as an end in itself, but as the means of achieving higher levels of being.

These neosocialist concerns were also shared by the Fascists and National Socialists. Combating the enervating and leveling effects of wealth and leisure, and edifying the character and taste of the masses, were the goals of *Dopolavoro* in Fascist Italy and Strength Through Joy in National Socialist Germany, as disquieting as this thought may be to socialists of the Left.

While it seems unlikely that Lovecraft was aware of this ideological tumult in European socialism, he arrived at similar conclusions in some key areas.

Lovecraft, like other writers who rejected Marxism, deemed both democracy and communism "fallacious for Western Civilization."[5] Instead, Lovecraft favored:

> . . . a kind of fascism which may, whilst helping the

---

it, albeit forgotten by most, stands as a permanent example of how a government can bypass private banking and issue its own credit.

[4] Erik Olssen, *John A. Lee* (Dunedin, New Zealand: University of Otago Press, 1977), p. 66.

[5] *H. P. Lovecraft: Selected Letters: 1932–1934*, vol. 4, ed. August Derleth and James Turner (Sauk City, Wis.: Arkham House, 1976), p. 93.

> dangerous masses at the expense of the needlessly rich, nevertheless preserves the essentials of traditional civilization and leaves political power in the hands of a small and cultivated (though not over-rich) governing class largely hereditary but subject to gradual increase as other individuals rise to its cultural level.[6]

Lovecraft feared that socialism, like capitalism, would pave the way for universal proletarianization and the consequent leveling of culture. Thus he proposed instead full employment and the shortening of the workday through mechanization under the guidance of a new socialist-fascist regime.

This again was probably a perceptive insight arrived at independently by Lovecraft, but it was very much a part of the new economic thinking of the time. In England, the Fabian socialist review, *The New Age*, edited by guild socialist A. R. Orage, became a forum for discussing Major C. H. Douglas' "Social Credit" theory, which was proposed as an alternative to the debt finance system, with the issue of a "social credit" to all citizens through a "National Dividend" allowing the full value of production to be consumed. They also aimed at using mechanization to decrease work hours and increase leisure, which they thought would be conducive to the blossoming of culture.

Both Ezra Pound and New Zealand poet Rex Fairburn were Social Crediters because they judged it the best economic system for the arts and culture. (These ideas have renewed relevance as the eight-hour workday, the long-fought gain of the early labor movement, is becoming a rarity.)

Lovecraft sought to eliminate the causes of social revo-

---

[6] Lovecraft, *Selected Letters,* vol. 4, p. 93.

lution, advocating the limitation of the vast accumulation of wealth, while recognizing the need to maintain wage disparities based on merit. His concern was the elimination of the "commercial oligarchs,"[7] which in practical terms was the purpose of Social Credit and of the neosocialists.

While regarding the primary goal of a nation to be the development of high aesthetic and intellectual standards, Lovecraft recognized that such a society must be based on the traditional social organization of "order, courage and endurance," his definition of civilization being that of a social organism devoted to "a high qualitative goal" maintained by the aforesaid ethos.

Lovecraft thought the hierarchical social order best fitted to the practicalities of the new machine age was a "fascistic one." The "demand-supply motive" would replace the profit motive in a state-directed economy that would reduce working hours while increasing leisure hours. The citizen could then be elevated culturally and intellectually as far as innate abilities allowed, "so that this leisure will be that of a civilized person rather than that of a cinema-haunting, dance-hall frequenting, pool-room loafing clod."

Lovecraft saw no wisdom in universal suffrage. He advocated a type of neo-aristocracy or meritocracy, with voting rights and the holding of public office "highly restricted." A technological, specialized civilization had rendered universal suffrage "a mockery and a jest." He wrote that, "People do not generally have the acumen to run a technological civilization effectively." This anti-democratic principle Lovecraft held to be true regardless

---

[7] Lovecraft, *Selected Letters: 1934–1937*, vol. 5, ed. August Derleth and James Turner (Sauk City, Wis.: Arkham House, 1976), p. 162.

of one's social or economic position, whether as menial laborer or as an academic.

The uninformed vote upon which democracy rests, Lovecraft wrote, "is a subject for uproarious cosmic laughter." The universal franchise meant that the unqualified, generally representing some "hidden interest," would assume office on the basis of having "the glibbest tongue" and "the flashiest catch-words."

His reference to "hidden interests" can only refer to his understanding of the oligarchic nature of democracy. This would have to be replaced by "a rational fascist government," where offices would require a prerequisite test of knowledge of economics, history, sociology, and business administration, although everyone—other than inassimilable aliens—would have the opportunity to apply.[8]

A year after Mussolini took power in 1922 Lovecraft wrote that, "Democracy is a false idol—a mere catchword and illusion of inferior classes, visionaries and dying civilizations." He saw in Fascist Italy "the sort of authoritative social and political control which alone produces things which make life worth living."

This was also why Ezra Pound admired Fascist Italy, writing: "Mussolini has told his people that poetry is a necessity *to the state*."[9] And: "I don't believe any estimate of Mussolini will be valid unless it starts from his passion for construction. Treat him as *artifex* and all the details fall into place. Take him as anything save the artist and you will get muddled with contradictions."[10]

---

[8] Lovecraft, *Selected Letters*, vol. 4, pp. 105–108.

[9] Quoted by E. Fuller Torrey, *The Roots of Treason: Ezra Pound and the Secrets of St. Elizabeths* (London: Sidgwick and Jackson, 1984), p. 138.

[10] Ezra Pound, *Jefferson and/or Mussolini* (1935) (New York: Liveright, 1970), pp. 33–34.

Such figures as Filippo Marinetti, Pound, and Lovecraft viewed Fascism as a movement that could successfully subordinate modern technological civilization to high art and culture, freeing the masses from a coarse and brutalizing commoditized popular culture.

Lovecraft thought the cosmos indifferent to mankind and concluded that the only meaning of human existence is to reach ever higher levels of mental and aesthetic development. But what Sir Oswald Mosley called actualization to *Higher Forms* in his post-war thinking,[11] and what Nietzsche called the goal of *Higher Man* and the *Overman*,[12] could not be achieved through "the low cultural standards of an underdeveloped majority. Such a civilization of mere working, eating, drinking, breeding, and vacantly loafing or childishly playing isn't worth maintaining." It is a form of lingering death and is particularly painful to the cultural elite.

Lovecraft was heavily influenced by Nietzsche and Oswald Spengler. Lovecraft recognized the organic, cyclic nature of cultural birth, youthfulness, maturity, senility, and death as the basis of the history of the rise and fall of civilizations. Thus the crisis brought to Western Civilization by the machine age was not unique. Lovecraft cites

---

11 Oswald Mosley, *Europe: Faith and Plan* (London: Euphorion, 1958), "The Doctrine of Higher Forms," pp. 143–47.

12 Friedrich Nietzsche, *Thus Spoke Zarathustra*, trans. R. J. Hollingdale (Middlesex: Penguin Books, 1975), "The Higher Man," pp. 296–305. A glimpse of Nietzschean philosophy is alluded to in Lovecraft's "Through the Gates of the Silver Key" where Randolph Carter discerns words from beyond the normal ken: "'The man of Truth is beyond good and evil,' intoned a voice that was not a voice. 'The man of Truth has ridden to All-Is-One . . .'" (Lovecraft, "Through the Gates of the Silver Key," *The Dream-Quest of Unknown Kadath* [New York: Ballantine Books, 1982], p. 189).

Spengler's *Decline of the West* as support for his view that civilization had reached the phase of "senility."[13]

Lovecraft saw cultural decline as a slow process spanning 500 to 1000 years. He sought a system that could overcome the cyclical laws of decay, which was also the motivation of Fascism.[14] Lovecraft believed it was possible to re-establish a new "equilibrium" over the course of 50 to 100 years, stating: "There is no need of worrying about civilization so long as the language and the general art tradition survives." The cultural tradition must be maintained above and beyond economic changes.[15]

In 1915 Lovecraft established his own political journal called *The Conservative,* which ran for 13 issues until 1923. The focus of the journal was defending high cultural standards, particularly in the field of letters, but it also opposed pacifism in favor of "moderate, healthy militarism" and "Pan-Saxonism," meaning "the domination of English and kindred races over the lesser divisions of mankind," and opposed anarchism and socialism.[16]

Like the neosocialists in Europe, Lovecraft opposed the materialistic conception of history as being equally bourgeois and Marxist. He saw Communism as "destroying the zest for life" for the sake of a theory.[17] Rejecting eco-

---

[13] Oswald Spengler, *The Decline of the West,* 2 vols., trans. Charles Francis Atkinson (London: George Allen and Unwin, 1971).

[14] "Fascism . . . was a movement to secure national renaissance by people who felt themselves threatened with decline into decadence and death and were determined to live, and to live greatly" (Oswald Mosley, *My Life* [London: Nelson, 1968], p. 287).

[15] Lovecraft, *Selected Letters,* vol. 4, p. 323.

[16] H. P. Lovecraft, "Editorial," *The Conservative,* vol. I, July 1915.

[17] Lovecraft, *Selected Letters,* vol. 4, p. 133.

nomic determinism as the primary motive of history, he saw "natural aristocrats" arising from all sectors of a population regardless of economic status. The aim of a society was to substitute "personal excellence for that of economic position"[18] which, despite Lovecraft's declared opposition to "socialism," is nonetheless essentially the same as the "ethical socialism" propounded by Hendrik de Man, Marcel Déat, *et al.* Lovecraft saw Fascism as an attempt to achieve this form of aristocracy in the context of modern industrial and technological society.

Lovecraft saw the pursuit of "equality" as a destructive rationale for an "atavistic revolt" against civilization by those who are uneasy with culture. The same motive was the root of Bolshevism, the French Revolution, the "back to nature" cult of Jean-Jacques Rousseau, and eighteenth-century Rationalism. Lovecraft saw that the same revolt was being taken up by "backward races" under the leadership of the Bolsheviks.[19]

These views are clearly Nietzschean, but they even more specifically resemble those of *The Revolt Against Civilization: The Menace of the Under-Man*[20] by the then popular author Lothrop Stoddard, whose work would certainly have attracted Lovecraft, with his concern for the maintenance and rebirth of civilization and his rejection of leveling creeds.

Although Lovecraft rejected egalitarianism, he did not advocate a tyranny that would repress the masses for the benefit of the few. Instead, he viewed elite rule as a necessary means for achieving the higher goals of cultural actualization. Lovecraft wished to see the elevation of the

---

18 Lovecraft, *Selected Letters*, vol. 5, pp. 330–33.

19 Lovecraft, *Selected Letters*, vol. 5, p. 245.

20 Lothrop Stoddard, *The Revolt Against Civilization: The Menace of the Under-Man* (London: Chapman and Hall, 1922).

greatest number possible.[21] Lovecraft also rejected class divisions as "vicious," whether emanating from the proletariat or the aristocracy. "Classes are something to be gotten rid of or minimized—not to be officially recognized." Lovecraft proposed to replace class conflict with an integral state that reflected the "general culture-stream." Between the individual and the state would exist a two-way loyalty.

Lovecraft regarded pacifism as an "evasion and idealistic hot air." He declared internationalism "a delusion and a myth."[22] He saw the League of Nations as "comic opera."[23] Wars are a constant in history and must be prepared for via universal conscription.[24] Historically war had strengthened the "national fiber," but mechanized warfare had negated the process; in fact the mass technological destruction of the First World War was widely recognized as dysgenic. Nonetheless the European, and specifically the Anglo-Saxon, must maintain his supremacy through firepower, for "a foeman's bullet is sweeter than a master's whip."[25] However, as one might expect from an anti-materialist, Lovecraft repudiated the typical modern cause of warfare, that of fighting for mercantile supremacy, "defense of one's own land and race [being] the proper object of armament."[26]

Lovecraft saw Jewish representation in the arts as responsible for what Francis Parker Yockey would call "culture distortion." New York City had been "completely Semiticized" and lost to the "national fabric." The Semitic

---

[21] Lovecraft, *Selected Letters,* vol. 4, pp. 104–105.

[22] Lovecraft, *Selected Letters,* vol. 5, pp. 311–12.

[23] Lovecraft, *Selected Letters,* vol. 4, pp. 15–16.

[24] Lovecraft, *Selected Letters,* vol. 4, p. 22.

[25] Lovecraft, *Selected Letters,* vol. 4, pp. 311–12.

[26] Lovecraft, *Selected Letters,* vol. 4, p. 31.

influence in literature, drama, finance, and advertising created an artificial culture and ideology "radically hostile to the virile American attitude." Like Yockey, Lovecraft saw the Jewish Question as a matter of an "antagonistic culture-tradition" rather than as a difference of race. Thus Jews could theoretically become assimilated into an American cultural tradition. The Negro problem, however, was one of biology and must be recognized by maintaining "an absolute color-line."[27]

This brief sketch is sufficient, I think, to show that H. P. Lovecraft belongs among an illustrious list of twentieth century creative geniuses—including W. B. Yeats, Ezra Pound, D. H. Lawrence, Knut Hamsun, Henry Williamson, Wyndham Lewis, and Yukio Mishima—whose rejection of materialism, egalitarianism, and cultural decadence caused them to search for a vital, hierarchical alternative to both capitalism and communism, a search that led them to entertain and embrace proto-fascist, fascist, or National Socialist ideas.

---

[27] Lovecraft, *Selected Letters,* vol. 4, pp. 193–95.

CHAPTER 3

GABRIELE D'ANNUNZIO

> "We artists are only then astonished witnesses of eternal aspirations, which help raise up our breed to its destiny."
>
> —Gabriele D'Annunzio[1]

GABRIELE D'ANNUNZIO, 1863–1938, a unique combination of artist and warrior, was born into a merchant family. He was a Renaissance man *par excellence*. This warrior bard was to have a crucial impact upon the rise of Fascism despite his not always being in accord with the way in which it developed.

EARLY LIFE

The lad who in later years was to be heavily influenced by Friedrich Nietzsche displayed an iron will at an early age. Learning to swim, he would go against the current or head for the biggest waves to discover his limits.[2] His career as a poet began early. At 16, he was known in Rome as an up-and-coming poet. At 19, D'Annunzio traveled to Rome, leading a bohemian lifestyle, working as a gossip columnist,[3] and writing his first novel *Il Piacere* (1889). A set of short stories followed, *Tales of the Pescara* (1884–86), celebrating the sensual and the violent. Then came his novel *Le Vergini Delle Rocce* (1895),[4] which was important because it introduced Italy to the ideal of the Nietzschean

---

[1] Anthony Rhodes, *The Poet as Superman: D'Annunzio* (London: Weidenfeld and Nicolson, 1959), p. 108.

[2] Rhodes, *The Poet as Superman*, p. 21.

[3] Rhodes, *The Poet as Superman*, pp. 25–26.

[4] Rhodes, *The Poet as Superman*, p. 48.

Overman. D'Annunzio's first visit to Greece in 1895 inspired him to write a national epic that he hoped would bring Italy into the twentieth century as a great nation. "I was to write a volume of poetic prose which will be a war cry of the Latin peoples." *Laus Vitae* expressed a pagan, Nietzschean ethos of "Desire, Voluptuousness, Pride, and Instinct, the imperial Quadriga."[5]

NEW IDEALS

Around this time, new ideals for the coming century were emerging, especially among young artists who were rejecting the bourgeois liberalism of the nineteenth century. In response to the comfort-seeking, security-conscious bourgeoisie and merchant-minded politicians, the young artists, writers, and poets were demanding nationalism and empire. They were represented by the Futurist movement with its provocative style and abrasive manifestos. Led by the poet Filippo Marinetti, the Futurists demanded a rejection of "pastism." They stood for a new age based on speed, dynamism, and martial valor.[6]

Within this tumult for a New Italy that rejected the bourgeois values of the nineteenth century, D'Annunzio wrote his play *La Nave* (1908) that celebrated the Venetian city-state of the Renaissance and called for action with the slogan: "Arm the prow and sail toward the wind."[7]

The impact of the play was so powerful that the actors came to real blows, and the populace of Rome shouted its slogans. The King congratulated D'Annunzio, and Aus-

---

[5] Rhodes, *The Poet as Superman*, p. 51. A *quadriga* is a four-horse chariot.

[6] Filippo Marinetti, "The Futurist Manifesto" and "Old Ideas Which Always Go Hand in Hand and Must be Separated," in Adrian Lyttelton, ed., *Italian Fascisms: From Pareto to Gentile* (London: Jonathan Cape, 1973).

[7] Rhodes, *The Poet as Superman*, p. 69.

tria officially protested to the Italian Foreign Office. D'Annunzio was now a major influence on Italian youth and on the Futurists. The climate created by D'Annunzio, the Futurists, and the Italian Nationalists enabled Prime Minister Francesco Crispi to embark upon imperial adventures in Africa, which culminated in the resurgence of an African Italian empire under Mussolini several decades later. D'Annunzio inspired both the general population and the Italian soldiers with his writings.

POLITICS

Although he did not fit into the conventional Left or Right—which can also be said of the emerging Italian nationalist movement—D'Annunzio entered Parliament in 1899 as a non-doctrinaire conservative with revolutionary ideas.[8] Nonetheless, he had contempt for Parliament and for parliamentarians as "the elected herd." He had written in 1895, "A State erected on the basis of popular suffrage and equality in voting, is not only ignoble, it is precarious. The State should always be no more than an institution for favoring the gradual elevation of a privileged class towards its ideal form of existence."[9]

He took his seat and forced a new election in 1900 by crossing the floor and joining with the Left to break a political impasse. He then stood for the Socialist Party, among whose leadership at the time was Mussolini,[10] although continuing to speak of a "national consciousness" that was contrary to the internationalism of the mainstream Socialists, as indeed Mussolini was to do.[11] Alt-

---

[8] Rhodes, *The Poet as Superman*, p. 79.

[9] D'Annunzio, *La Vergini della Rocce* (1895).

[10] Margherita G. Sarfatti, *The Life of Benito Mussolini* (London: Thornton Butterworth, 1925), pp. 162–200.

[11] Sarfatti, *The Life of Benito Mussolini*, pp. 207–12.

hough he was not re-elected, D'Annunzio had contributed to the formation of an ideological synthesis, along with the nationalists and the Futurists, that was several decades later to transcend both Left and Right and emerge as Fascism. D'Annunzio expressed the new synthesis of the coming politics thus: "Everything in life depends upon the eternally new. Man must either renew himself or die."

THE FIRST WORLD WAR

D'Annunzio was living in France when the war broke out.[12] He visited the front and resolved to return to Italy to agitate for his country's entry into the war. Like Mussolini and Marinetti, D'Annunzio saw the war as an opportunity for Italy to take her place among the great powers of the twentieth century. D'Annunzio was invited to speak before a crowd at an official opening of the Garibaldi monument, declaring his own "Sermon on the Mount":

> Blessed are they, who having yesterday cried against this event, will today accept the supreme necessity, and do not wish to be the Last but the First! Blessed are the young who, starved of glory, shall be satisfied! Blessed are the merciful, for they shall be called on to quench a splendid flow of blood, and dress a wonderful wound . . .[13]

The crowd was ecstatic.

At 52 and considered a national treasure, having re-established an Italian national literature, there was pressure to dissuade him from enlisting in the army, but he was commissioned in the Novara Lancers and saw more than 50 actions. Such was the daring of his ventures that Italy's leading literary figure soon became her greatest

---

[12] Rhodes, *The Poet as Superman*, p. 141.

[13] Rhodes, *The Poet as Superman*, p. 147.

war hero. He flew many times over the Alps at a time when such a feat was considered extraordinary. The Austrians put a bounty on his head. He responded by entering Buccari harbor with a small band of handpicked men in a motorboat, firing his torpedoes, and leaving behind rubber containers, each containing a lyrical message in indelible ink.

D'Annunzio was especially noted for his air excursions over enemy lines dropping propaganda leaflets. It was during a bombing flight over Pola that he and his airmen first used the war cry "Eja! Eja! Eja! Alala!"[14] This was said to be the cry used by Achilles to spur on his horses. It was later adapted by D'Annunzio's legionaries when they took Fiume and eventually by the Fascists. After serious damage to an eye, he was told not to fly again, but within several months had returned to the air and was awarded a silver medal.

He then slogged it out on foot in the assault from Castagna to the sea. He returned from the war an international hero, having been awarded a gold medal, five silver medals, a bronze medal, and the officer's cross of the Savoy Military Order. He also received the Military Cross from Britain, with many other countries adding to his honors.

FIUME

After the Allied victory, Italy did not receive the rewards she had expected. Fiume was a particular point of contention. Venetian in culture and history, the port city

---

[14] Rhodes, *The Poet as Superman*, p. 161, n1. Interestingly, this war cry was revived in 1985 by the Slovenian "collectivist" industrial music group Laibach in the lyrics of "Nova Akropola," a clear tribute to D'Annunzzio's Pola air raid. See New Collectivism, *Neue Slowenische Kunst*, trans. Marjan Golobič (Los Angeles: Amok Books, 1991).

had been occupied by the French, English, American, and Italian troops; yet the Italian government favored turning its administration over to Yugoslavia. Mussolini, Marinetti, and D'Annunzio again joined forces to agitate on the common theme that Italy should annex Fiume. Young officers formed an army with the motto: "Fiume or death!" D'Annunzio was asked to lead an expedition to take the city for Italy.

At dawn on September 12, 1919, D'Annunzio marched off at the head of a column of 287 veterans. As they marched through Italy towards Fiume, they picked up soldiers and supplies along the way. By the time D'Annunzio reached the city, he had gathered an army of 1,000. D'Annunzio confronted General Vittorio Emanuele Pittaluga, the Italian commander of the city, and, pointing to his medals declared, "Fire first on this." The General's eyes filled with tears, and he replied: "Great poet! I do not wish to be the cause of spilling Italian blood. I am honored to meet you for the first time. May your dream be fulfilled."[15] The two embraced and entered Fiume together. Once D'Annunzio had taken Fiume, others from all over Italy flocked to him, including nationalists, anarchists, Futurists, syndicalists, soldiers, and men of the arts. "In this mad and vile world, Fiume is the symbol of liberty," declared D'Annunzio.[16]

However, the Free State was not completely isolated in the world and caught the imagination of others outside Italy who desired to see the overthrow of the bourgeois order. Soviet Russia granted official recognition to the Free State. The day after the seizure of Fiume, the Dada Club in Berlin sent a telegram to *Corriere della Sera* stating: "Conquest a great Dadaist action, and will employ all

---

[15] Rhodes, *The Poet as Superman*, pp. 175–77.

[16] Rhodes, *The Poet as Superman*, p. 179.

means to ensure its recognition. The Dadaist world atlas Dadaco already recognises Fiume as an Italian city." Günter Berghaus has written:

> Between December 1919 and December 1920 Fiume became a little world of its own, a little microcosm where radical dreams and aspirations were given an unprecedented opportunity to be lived out and experimented with. . . . Groups of revolutionary intellectuals managed to assume control over the city and created a political culture where spontaneous expression of beliefs replaced the tedious procedures of parliamentary democracy. Artistic fantasy and energy gave birth to a new "aesthetics" of communal life where the fusion of political and artistic *avant-garde* became a reality. A festive lifestyle replaced conventional social behaviour.[17]

Although D'Annunzio's Fiume has often been regarded as the forerunner of Fascism, the atmosphere, organization, and aesthetics of the Free State suggest a synthesis of the Renaissance, Futurism, and syndicalism, which drew the support of an eclectic bunch of rebels. The contemporary anarchist writer Hakim Bey has called Fiume the first "temporary autonomous zone," run on "pirate economics," and based on an "intensity of living."[18]

A Renaissance City-State

D'Annunzio recreated Fiume as a twentieth-century Renaissance city-state. It would be the catalyst for a

---

[17] Günter Berghaus, *Futurism and Politics: Between Anarchist Rebellion and Fascist Reaction, 1909–1944* (Oxford: Berghahn Books, 1995), p. 139.

[18] Hakim Bey, *T.A.Z. The Temporary Autonomous Zone, Ontological Anarchy, Poetic Terrorism* (Brooklyn: Autonomedia, 1985).

"League of Oppressed Nations" to counter the League of Nations of the bourgeois powers.[19] The Free State of Fiume was proclaimed with the *Statute of the Carnaro*, co-authored by D'Annunzio and the revolutionary syndicalist Alceste de Ambris, attesting to the Fiume venture as being the harbinger of the revolutionary syndicalist and nationalist synthesis that gave birth to Fascism.

The *Statute of the Carnaro* instituted physical training for youth, old age pensions, universal education, aesthetic instruction, and unemployment relief. Private property was recognized but on the condition of its "proper, continuous, and efficient use." Corporations and guilds after the medieval manner were established to represent workers and producers in place of the old political parties. Both freedom of religion and atheism were protected. A College of Ediles would be "elected with discernment from men of taste and education," who would maintain aesthetic standards in the architecture and construction of the city-state. The parliament, or Council of the Best, was enjoined to minimize chatter, with sessions held with "notably concise brevity." A higher chamber was called the Council of Providers. D'Annunzio oversaw the whole edifice as the *Commandante*. Music was elevated as "a religious and social institution" by statute.[20] For 15 months, the *Commandante* held out against Allied protests and the blockade erected by the Italian government.

BLOCKADE

The Italian government eventually tightened its blockade, which resulted in food shortages at the time of the Eu-

---

[19] Rhodes, *The Poet as Superman*, p. 183.

[20] Gabriele D'Annunzio and Alceste de Ambris, "The Constitution of Fiume," September 8, 1920, in Roger Griffin, ed., *Fascism* (Oxford: Oxford University Press, 1995), pp. 35–37.

ropean-wide influenza epidemic. To counter the blockade, D'Annunzio formed the *Uscocchi* (from an old Adriatic name for a type of pirate), who captured ships, robbed warehouses, and stole coal, arms, meat, coffee, and ammunition, even army horses, in daring raids all over Italy.[21]

D'Annunzio planned to march on Rome and take the entire country. Indeed, the legionary's song had the refrain, "with the bomb and the dagger we will enter the Quirinale."[22] D'Annunzio had hoped for the support of Mussolini's Fascists, who had been propagandizing for D'Annunzio's occupation of Fiume,[23] but Mussolini considered such a march on Rome premature, and possibly looked upon D'Annunzio as a rival to his own aims.

Italian troops now moved on Fiume. D'Annunzio ordered a general mobilization. He hoped that Italian troops would not fire on fellow Italians. Such a notion was repugnant to D'Annunzio, as it had been to General Pittaluga when he gave way to D'Annunzio's occupation. Military operations began on December 24, 1920, "the Christmas of Blood" as D'Annunzio called it. Twenty thousand troops began to move against D'Annunzio's 3,000. The *Andrea Dona* sailed within firing range. D'Annunzio was given an ultimatum to surrender or suffer bombardment. After the shelling began, the women of the city came forth on the balconies holding aloft their babies, shouting, "This one Italy! Take this one. But not D'Annunzio!"

The *Commandante* gathered his cabinet together and announced his capitulation. Although his men had repulsed the government's troops for five days, the city

---

21 Rhodes, *The Poet as Superman*, pp. 190–200.

22 The Quirinal Palace in Rome was then the official residence of the King of Italy. It is now the official residence of the President of the Italian Republic. — Ed.

23 Sarfatti, *The Life of Benito Mussolini*, pp. 269–270.

could not withstand heavy shelling. "I cannot impose on this heroic city its ruin and certain destruction," said D'Annunzio.[24]

FASCISM

D'Annunzio retired to a secluded house he called "The Shrine of Italian Victories." He resumed his writing. He remained the most popular figure in Italy whom both Fascists and anti-Fascists tried to recruit. Despite what he considered Mussolini's betrayal over Fiume, he refused to assist the anti-Fascists. On October 27, 1922, the Fascists marched on Rome. The new regime was established on a more realistic and pragmatic basis than the romantic and visionary ideals that D'Annunzio had briefly realized at Fiume.

Many of the trappings of the Fascist movement were first used by D'Annunzio, including the revival of the Roman salute and the wearing of the blackshirt. Mussolini adopted D'Annunzio's style of speaking to the populace from balconies with the crowds responding. Italy was organized as a Corporate (guild) state as Fiume had been, and cultural figures were especially esteemed.

In 1924, most of Fiume was secured from Yugoslavia. This and the withdrawal from the League of Nations, and in particular the invasion of Abyssinia, drew D'Annunzio closer to Mussolini.[25] Although he refrained from participation in public life, the regime showered D'Annunzio with honors, made him a prince, published his collected works, and made him an honorary general of the air force and president of the Italian Academy.[26] On March 1, 1938, D'Annunzio died suddenly of a cerebral hemorrhage. At

---

[24] Rhodes, *The Poet as Superman*, p. 220.

[25] Rhodes, *The Poet as Superman*, p. 236.

[26] Rhodes, *The Poet as Superman*, p. 233.

D'Annunzio's funeral, Mussolini said: "You may be sure Italy will arrive at the summit you dreamed of."[27]

The legacy of the Free City of Fiume became an important part of the Fascist mythos. Mussolini as editor of *Il Popolo d'Italia* gave Fiume moral support and also launched a subscription to give financial support. But at the time of the bombardment of Fiume, D'Annunzio's desperate efforts to get Fascist support failed. From a Fascist perspective the venture would have been considered heroic but unrealistic, and the Fascists were not then in a position to stage a revolt. Margherita Sarfatti writes of "the beacon of the Adriatic had been extinguished in blood. Fiume had been taken and evacuated, the *Commandante* had been wounded, and, brother fighting against brother, forty legionaries had fallen at the hands of their brother-soldiers of Italy."[28]

Mussolini however responded that at no time had he indicated the Fascists would be in a position to launch a revolution in the event of Fiume being attacked: "Revolution will be accomplished with the army, not against the army; with arms, not without them; with trained forces, not with undisciplined mobs called together in the streets. It will succeed when it is surrounded by a halo of sympathy by the majority, and if it has not that, it will fail."[29]

Mussolini saw in the legionaries that dispersed from Fiume and scattered throughout Italy the inspiration for a New Italy and the cause of Fiume. "On 3rd of March, 1924, Mussolini was to sign the treaty of annexation whereby Fiume was joined to the kingdom of Italy!"[30]

---

[27] Rhodes, *The Poet as Superman*, p. 242.
[28] Sarfatti, *The Life of Benito Mussolini*, p. 280.
[29] Sarfatti, *The Life of Benito Mussolini*, p. 281.
[30] Sarfatti, *The Life of Benito Mussolini*, p. 282.

CHAPTER 4

FILIPPO MARINETTI

FILIPPO TOMMASO MARINETTI, 1876–1944, is unlike most of the post-nineteenth century cultural *avant-garde,* who rebelled against liberalism, rationalism, and industrialism, as well as the rise of the democratic masses and the rule of the moneyed elite. His revolt against the modern world did not hark back to a perceived "golden age," such as the medieval era upheld by W. B. Yeats and Julius Evola. Nor did he reject technology in favor of a return to a simpler, agrarian form of life, as advocated by Henry Williamson and Knut Hamsun. On the contrary, Marinetti embraced the new facts of technology—the machine, speed, dynamic energy—in a movement called Futurism.

The Futurist response to the facts of the new age is therefore a quite unique reaction from the anti-liberal literati and artists. Futurism, moreover, continues to influence certain aspects of industrial and post-industrial subcultures.[1]

Marinetti was born in Alexandria, Egypt, in 1876. He graduated in law in Genoa in 1899. Although the political and philosophical aspects of his studies held his interest, he

---

[1] An example of a contemporary cultural movement analogous to Futurism is Neue Slowenische Kunst, which like Futurism embraces music, graphic arts, architecture, and drama. It is a movement whose influence is felt beyond the borders of Slovenia. The best-known manifestation of its aesthetic is the industrial music group Laibach. See New Collectivism, *Neue Slowenische Kunst,* trans. Marjan Golobič (Los Angeles: Amok Books, 1991).

A specifically neo-Futurist movement, aborted by the suicide of its founder, was Sarote Industries. This writer's collection of Sarote and "Book and Sword" memorabilia was donated to the Sarote Industries Memorial Website: http://www.sarote.org/

traveled frequently between France and Italy, and interested himself in the *avant-garde* arts of the late nineteenth century, promoting young poets in both countries. He was already a strong critic of the conservative and traditional approaches of Italian poets. He was at this time an enthusiast for the modern, revolutionary music of Richard Wagner, seeing it as assailing "equilibrium and sobriety . . . meditation and silence . . ."[2]

By 1904, Futurist elements had manifested in his writing, particularly in his poem "Destruction" that he called "an erotic and anarchist poem," a eulogy to the "avenging sea" as a symbol of revolution. After an apocalyptic destruction, the process of rebuilding begins on the ruins of the "Old World." Here already is the praise of death as dynamic and transformative.[3]

With the death of Marinetti's father in 1907, his inheritance allowed him to travel widely, and he became a well-known cultural figure throughout Europe.[4] Nietzsche was at this time one of the most well-known intellectuals who desired liberation from the old order. Nietzsche was widely read among the literati of Italy, and Marinetti's future colleague, Gabriele D'Annunzio, was his most prominent exponent.[5]

Among the other philosophers of particular importance whom Marinetti studied was the French syndicalist theorist

---

[2] Günter Berghaus, *Futurism and Politics: Between Anarchist Rebellion and Fascist Reaction, 1909–1944* (Oxford: Berghahn Books, 1996), p. 18.

[3] Berghaus, *Futurism and Politics*, p. 20.

[4] He became a millionaire. See Richard Jensen, "Futurism and Fascism," *History Today*, vol. 45, no. 11, November 1995, p. 36.

[5] It was D'Annunzio's novel *Le Vergini delle Rocce* that introduced Italians to Nietzsche's ideal of the Overman. See Anthony Rhodes, *The Poet as Superman: D'Annunzio* (London: Weidenfeld and Nicholson, 1959), p. 48.

Georges Sorel.[6] Sorelian syndicalism rejected Marxism in favor of a society comprised of small productive, cooperative units or syndicates. Sorel also founded a new myth of heroic action and struggle. Eschewing the pacifism of the Left, Sorel viewed war as a dynamic of human action. Sorel in turn was himself influenced by Nietzsche, and applying the Nietzschean Overman to socialism, states that the working class revolution requires heroic leaders.

Sorel became influential not only among Left-wing syndicalists but also among certain radical nationalists in both France and Italy. A manifestation of this was the Proudhon Circle in France comprising Maurrassian Rightist monarchists and Sorelian revolutionary syndicalists, and named after the so-called "father of anarchism," in a synthesis that was to give rise to Fascism in that country at the same time as it appeared in Italy.[7]

THE FUTURIST MANIFESTO

Marinetti's artistic ideas crystallized in the Futurist movement that originated from a meeting of artists and musicians in Milan in 1909 to draft a Futurist Manifesto.[8] With Marinetti were Carlo Carrà, Umberto Boccioni, Luigi Russolo, and Gino Severini. The manifesto was first published February 20, 1909 in the Parisian paper *Le Figaro*,[9] and exhorted youth to, "Sing the love of danger, the habit of energy and boldness." The initial movement drew the

---

[6] Berghaus, *Futurism and Politics*, p. 25.

[7] Zeev Sternhell, *Neither Left nor Right: Fascist Ideology in France*, trans. David Maisel (Princeton: Princeton University Press, 1996). The situation is ironic, given the vigor with which present-day adolescent bourgeois "anarchists" try to attack anything of an even vaguely Rightist or "fascist" nature.

[8] Berghaus, *Futurism and Politics*, p. 9.

[9] Adrian Lyttelton, ed., *Italian Fascisms: From Pareto to Gentile* (London: Jonathan Cape, 1975), p. 207.

interest of anarchists and syndicalists of the non-orthodox Left which sought a revolt against bourgeois democratic "safety."[10]

In 1913 the Futurist Political Program was published, which served as the basis for the establishment of the Futurist Political Party in 1918; that is, after Marinetti had undertaken a campaign for Italian entry in the World War, along with Mussolini and D'Annunzio.

The First Fascist Congress was held in Florence in 1919, and Marinetti remarked that the atmosphere was thoroughly Futurist in sentiment, but an electoral pact between the Futurists and the Fascists was abortive, and Marinetti insisted on adhering to the radical Left, while he maintained a large element of support among the Fascists.[11]

In contrast to those Fascists and nationalists who sought inspiration from Classical Rome, the Futurists were contemptuous of all tradition, of all that is past: "We want to exult aggressive motion . . . we affirm that the magnificence of the world has been enriched by a new beauty: the beauty of speed."[12]

The machine was poetically eulogized. The racing car became the icon of the new epoch, "which seems to run on machine-gun fire."[13] The Futurist aesthetic was to be joy in violence and war, as "the only cure for the world." Motion, dynamic energy, action, and heroism were the foundations of the culture of the Futurist future. The fisticuffs, the sprint, and the kick were expressions of culture. The Futur-

---

[10] For the ideological crisis in the Left in France and Italy resulting from dissatisfaction with the Marxian materialist conception of history, see Sternhell, *Neither Left nor Right.*

[11] Berghaus, *Futurism and Politics,* p. 9.

[12] Marinetti, "The Futurist Manifesto," Point 4 (1909), *Italian Fascisms,* p. 211.

[13] Marinetti, "The Futurist Manifesto," Point 4 (1909), *Italian Fascisms,* p. 211.

ist Manifesto is as much a challenge to the political and social order as it is to the *status quo* in the arts.

It declared:

1. We want to sing the love of danger, the habit of energy and rashness.

2. The essential elements of our poetry will be courage, audacity, and revolt.

3. Literature has up to now magnified pensive immobility, ecstasy, and slumber. We want to exalt movements of aggression, feverish sleeplessness, the double march, the perilous leap, the slap, and the blow with the fist.

4. We declare that the splendour of the world has been enriched by a new beauty: the beauty of speed. A racing automobile with its bonnet adorned with great tubes like serpents with explosive breath . . . a roaring motor car which seems to run on machine-gun fire, is more beautiful than the Victory of Samothrace.

5. We want to sing the man at the wheel, the ideal axis of which crosses the earth, itself hurled along its orbit.

6. The poet must spend himself with warmth, glamour, and prodigality to increase the enthusiastic fervour of the primordial elements.

7. Beauty exists only in struggle. There is no masterpiece that has not an aggressive character. Poetry must be a violent assault on the forces of the unknown, to force them to bow before man.

8. We are on the extreme promontory of the centuries! What is the use of looking behind at the moment when we must open the mysterious shutters of the impossible? Time and Space died yesterday. We are already living in the absolute, since we have already created eternal, omnipresent speed.

9. We want to glorify war—the only cure for the world—militarism, patriotism, the destructive gesture of the anarchists, the beautiful ideas which kill, and contempt for women.

10. We want to demolish museums and libraries, fight morality, feminism, and all opportunist or utilitarian cowardice.

11. We will sing of great crowds agitated by work, pleasure, and revolt; the multi-coloured and polyphonic surf of revolutions in the modern capitals: the nocturnal vibration of the arsenals and the workshops beneath their violent electric moons: the gluttonous railway stations devouring smoking serpents; factories suspended from the clouds by the thread of their smoke; bridges with the leap of gymnasts flung across the diabolic cutlery of sunny rivers: adventurous steamers sniffing the horizon; great-breasted locomotives, puffing on the rails like enormous steel horses with long tubes for bridles, and the gliding flight of aeroplanes whose propellers sound like the flapping of a flag and the applause of enthusiastic crowds.

It is in Italy that we are issuing this manifesto of ruinous and incendiary violence, by which we today are founding Futurism, because we want to deliver Italy from its gangrene of professors, archeologists, tourist guides, and antiquaries.

Italy has been too long the great second-hand market. We want to get rid of the innumerable museums which cover it with innumerable cemeteries.

Museums, cemeteries! Truly identical in their sinister juxtaposition of bodies that do not know each other. Public dormitories where you sleep side by side forever with beings you hate or do not know. Reciprocal ferocity of the painters and sculptors who murder each other in the same museum with blows of line and colour. To make a visit once a year, as one goes to see the graves of our dead once a year, that we could allow! We can even imagine placing flowers once a year at the feet of the Gioconda! But to take our sadness, our fragile courage, and our anxiety to the museum every day, that we cannot admit! Do you want to poison yourselves? Do you want to rot?

What can you find in an old picture except the painful contortions of the artist trying to break uncrossable barriers which obstruct the full expression of his dream?

To admire an old picture is to pour our sensibility into a funeral urn instead of casting it forward with violent spurts of action and creation. Do you want to waste the best part of your strength in a useless admiration of the past, from which you emerge exhausted, diminished, trampled on?

Indeed, daily visits to museums, libraries, and academies (those cemeteries of wasted effort, calvaries of crucified dreams, registers of false starts!) is for artists what prolonged supervision by the parents is for intelligent young men, drunk with the own talent and ambition.

For the dying, for invalids, and for prisoners it may be all right. It is, perhaps, some sort of balm for their wounds, the admirable past, at a moment when the future is denied them. But we will have none of it, we, the young, strong, and living Futurists!

Let the good incendiaries with charred fingers come! Here they are! Heap up the fire to the shelves of the libraries! Divert the canals to flood the cellars of the museums! Let the glorious canvases swim ashore! Take the picks and hammers! Undermine the foundation of venerable towns!

The oldest of us are not yet thirty years old: we have

therefore at least ten years to accomplish our task. When we are forty, let younger and stronger men than we throw us in the wastepaper-basket like useless manuscripts! They will come against us from afar, leaping on the light cadence of their first poems, clutching the air with their predatory fingers and sniffing at the gates of the academies the good scent of our decaying spirits, already promised to the catacombs of the libraries.

But we shall not be there. They will find us at last one winter's night in the depths of the country in a sad hangar echoing with the notes of the monotonous rain, crouched near our trembling aeroplanes, warming our hands at the wretched fire which our books of today will make when they flame gaily beneath the glittering flight of their pictures.

They will crowd around us, panting with anguish and disappointment, and exasperated by our proud indefatigable courage, will hurl themselves forward to kill us, with all the more hatred as their hearts will be drunk with love and admiration for us. And strong healthy Injustice will shine radiantly from their eyes. For art can only be violence, cruelty, and injustice.

The oldest among us are not yet thirty, yet we have already wasted treasures, treasures of strength, love, courage, and keen will, hastily, deliriously, without thinking, with all our might, till we are out of breath.

Look at us! We are not out of breath, our hearts are not in the least tired. For they are nourished by fire, hatred, and speed! Does that surprise you? It is because you do not even remember having been alive! Standing on the world's summit, we launch once more our challenge to the stars!

Your objections? All right! I know them! Of course! We know just what our beautiful false intelligence af-

> firms: "We are only the sum and the prolongation of our ancestors," it says. Perhaps! All right! What does it matter? But we will not listen! Take care not to repeat those infamous words! Instead, lift up your head!
>
> Standing on the word's summit we launch once again our insolent challenge to the stars![14]

A plethora of manifestos by Marinetti and his colleagues followed, encompassing Futurist cinema, painting, music ("noise"), and prose, as well as their political and sociological implications.

WAR: THE WORLD'S ONLY HYGIENE

Marinetti's manifesto on war,[15] written in the same manner as his manifesto to students the previous year,[16] shows the central place of violence and conflict in the Futurist doctrine:

> We Futurists, who for over two years, scorned by the Lame and Paralyzed, have glorified the love of danger and violence, praised patriotism and war, the hygiene of the world, are happy to finally experience this great Futurist hour of Italy, while the foul tribe of pacifists huddles dying in the deep cellars of the ridiculous palace at The Hague.
>
> We have recently had the pleasure of fighting in the streets with the most fervent adversaries of the war and shouting in their faces our firm beliefs:

---

14 Marinetti, "Manifesto of Futurism," *Italian Fascisms*, pp. 211–15.

15 As it was to have in the syndicalist movement under the influence of Sorel. See Sternhell, *Neither Left nor Right*.

16 Marinetti, "The War as the Catharsis of Italian Society," November 29, 1914, in Roger Griffin, ed., *Fascism* (Oxford: Oxford University Press, 1995), pp. 25–26.

1. All liberties should be given to the individual and the collectivity, save that of being cowardly.

2. Let it be proclaimed that the word *Italy* should prevail over the word *Freedom*.

3. Let the tiresome memory of Roman greatness be canceled by an Italian greatness a hundred times greater.

For us today, Italy has the shape and power of a fine Dreadnought battleship with its squadron of torpedo-boat islands. Proud to feel that the martial fervor throughout the nation is equal to ours, we urge the Italian government, Futurist at last, to magnify all the national ambitions, disdaining the stupid accusations of piracy, and proclaim the birth of Pan-Italianism.

Futurist poets, painters, sculptors, and musicians of Italy! As long as the war lasts let us set aside our verse, our brushes, scapulas, and orchestras! The red holidays of genius have begun! There is nothing for us to admire today but the dreadful symphonies of the shrapnel and the mad sculptures that our inspired artillery molds among the masses of the enemy.[17]

Artistic Storm Trooper

Marinetti brought his dynamic character into an aggressive campaign to promote Futurism. The Futurists aimed to aggravate society out of bourgeois complacency and safe existence through innovative street theater, abrasive art, speeches, and manifestos. The speaking style of Marinetti was itself bombastic and thunderous. The art was aggravating to conventional society and the art establishment. If a painting was of a man with a moustache, the whiskers would be depicted with the bristles of a shaving brush

---

[17] Marinetti, "War: The World's Only Hygiene," 1915.

pasted onto the canvas. A train would be depicted with the words "puff, puff."

Both the words and deeds of the Futurists matched the nature of the art in expressing contempt for the *status quo* with its preoccupation with "pastism" or the "*passé*." Marinetti, for example, described Venice as "a city of dead fish and decaying houses, inhabited by a race of waiters and touts."

To the Futurist Umberto Boccioni, Dante, Beethoven, and Michelangelo were "sickening," whilst Carlo Carrà set about painting sounds, noises, and even smells. Marinetti traversed Europe giving interviews, arranging exhibitions, meetings, and dinners. Vermilion posters with huge block letters spelling "Futurism" were plastered throughout Italy on factories, in dance halls, cafés, and town squares.

Futurist performances were organized to provoke riots. Glue was put onto seats. Two tickets for the same seat would be sold to provoke a fight. "Noise music" would blare while poetry or manifestos were recited and paintings shown. Fruit and rotten spaghetti would be thrown from the audience, and the performances would usually end in brawls.

Marinetti replied to jeers with humor. He ate the fruit thrown at him. He welcomed the hostility as proving that Futurism was not appealing to the mediocre.[18]

POLITICS

The first political contacts of Marinetti and the Futurists were from the Left rather than the Right, despite Marinetti's extreme nationalism and call for war as the "hygiene of mankind, and his support for Italy's embryonic neo-imperial adventures, supporting the Italian invasion of

---

18 Jensen, "Futurism and Fascism," p. 37.

Libya in 1912."[19] There were syndicalists and anarchists who shared Marinetti's views on the energizing and revolutionary nature of war and gave him a reception.

In 1909, Marinetti entered the general elections and issued a "First Political Manifesto" which is anti-clerical and states that the only Futurist political program is "national pride," calling for the elimination of pacifism and the representatives of the old order. During that year, Marinetti was heavily involved in agitating for Italian sovereignty over Austrian-ruled Trieste. The political alliance with the extreme Left began with the anarcho-syndicalist Ottavio Dinale,[20] whose paper reprinted the Futurist Manifesto. The paper, *La demolizione* was of a general combative nature, aiming to unite into one "fascio" all those of revolutionary tendencies, to "oppose with full energy the inertia and indolence that threatens to suffocate all life." The phrase is distinctly Futurist.

Marinetti announced that he intended to campaign politically as both a syndicalist and a nationalist, a synthesis that would eventually arise in Fascism. In 1910, he forged links with the Italian Nationalist Association,[21] which had a pro-labor, syndicalist program.[22] In 1913, a Futurist political manifesto was issued which called for enlargement of the military, an "aggressive foreign policy," colonial expansionism, and "pan-Italianism"; a "cult" of progress, speed, and heroism; opposition to the nostalgia for monuments, ruins, and museums; economic protectionism, anti-

---

[19] Jensen, "Futurism and Fascism," p. 37.

[20] Berghaus, *Futurism and Politics*, pp. 54–55.

[21] Berghaus, *Futurism and Politics*, p. 59.

[22] Enrico Corradini, "The Principles of Nationalism," Report to the First Nationalist Congress, Florence, December 3, 1910, in *Italian Fascisms*, pp. 146–48. "Italy is, materially and morally, a proletarian nation." See also Corradini's "The Proletarian Nations and Nationalism" (1911), *Italian Fascisms*, pp. 148–51.

socialism, and anti-clericalism. The movement generated wide enthusiasm among university students.[23]

INTERVENTION

The chance for Italy's "place in the sun" came with World War I. Not only the nationalists were demanding Italy's entry into the war, but so too were certain revolutionary syndicalists and a faction of socialists led by Mussolini. From the literati came D'Annunzio and Marinetti.

In a manifesto addressed to students in 1914, Marinetti states the purpose of Futurism and calls for intervention in the war. Futurism was the "doctor" to cure Italy of "pastism," a remedy "valid for any country." The "ancestor-cult far from cementing the race" was making Italians "anemic and putrid." Futurism was now "being fully realized in the great world war."

His exhortation to Italian students to demand Italy's place in the world via participation in the World War, provided an added poetical and romantic aspect to the interventionist campaign that was also taken up by D'Annunzio.

However, far from drawing from Italy's Roman heritage, Marinetti damned the great past as a hindrance to a greater future. His manifesto to students provides an insight into Marinetti's revolutionary repudiation of "pastism," because "an illustrious past was crushing Italy and an infinitely more glorious future."

This "pastism" was condemned along with "archaeology, academicism, senilism, quietism, the obsession with sex, the tourist industry, etc. "Our ultra-violent, anti-clerical, and anti-traditionalist nationalism is based on the inexhaustibility of Italian blood and the struggle against the ancestor-cult, which, far from cementing the race,

[23] Marinetti, "Political Program of Futurism," October 11, 1913.

makes it anemic and putrid."[24]

Marinetti, like many syndicalists who broke from the internationalist outlook of orthodox socialism, saw the war as a revolutionary cause,[25] describing it as "the most beautiful Futurist poem which has so far been seen." Futurism itself was artistic warfare, and "the militarization of innovating artists." The war as a revolutionary act would sweep from power all the decrepit representatives of the past:

> diplomats, professors, philosophers, archaeologists, critics, cultural obsession, Greek, Latin, history, senilism, museums, libraries, the tourist industry. The War will promote gymnastics, sport, practical schools of agriculture, business, and industrialists. The War will rejuvenate Italy, will enrich her with men of action, will force her to live no longer off the past, off ruins and the mild climate, but off her own national forces.[26]

According to Richard Jensen, the Futurists were probably the first to organize pro-war protests.[27] Mussolini and Marinetti held their first joint meeting in Milan on March 31, 1915. In April, both were arrested in Rome for organizing a demonstration.

Futurists were no mere windbags. The Futurists were among the first to enlist for active service.[28] Nearly all distinguished themselves in the war, as did Mussolini and

---

[24] Marinetti, "The War as the Catharsis of Italian Society."

[25] Mussolini, "Courage," *Il Popolo d'Italia*, November 15, 1914 and "The War as a Revolutionary Event," in Griffin, *Fascism*, pp. 26–28.

[26] Marinetti, "The War as the Catharsis of Italian Society."

[27] Jensen, "Futurism and Fascism," p. 37.

[28] Berghaus, *Futurism and Politics*, p. 81.

D'Annunzio. The Futurist architect Antonio Sant'Elia was killed, as was Umberto Boccioni.[29] Marinetti enlisted with the Alpini regiment and was wounded and decorated for valor.

THE FUTURIST PARTY

In 1918, Marinetti began directing his attention to a new postwar Italy. He published a manifesto announcing the Futurist Political Party, the name of which, interestingly, was the Fasci Politici Futuristi. The manifesto, an elaboration of Marinetti's Futurist Political Manifesto of 1913, called for "revolutionary nationalism" for both imperialism and social revolution. "We must carry our war to total victory."

Demands of the manifesto included the eight hour day and equal pay for women, the nationalization and redistribution of land to veterans; heavy taxes on acquired and inherited wealth; the gradual abolition of marriage through easy divorce; a strong Italy freed from nostalgia, tourists, and priests; and the industrialization and modernization of "moribund cities" that live as tourist centers. A corporatist policy called for the abolition of parliament and its replacement with a technical government of 30 or 40 young directors elected form the trade associations.[30]

The Futurist party concentrated its propaganda on the soldiers[31] and recruited many war veterans of the elite Arditi (daredevils), the black-shirted shock troops of the army who would charge into battle stripped to the waist, a grenade in each hand and a dagger between their teeth. While the program was too extreme for popular appeal, it did win

---

29 Berghaus, *Futurism and Politics*, p. 83.

30 Marinetti, "Manifesto of the Futurist Political Party," September 1918, in Griffin, *Fascism*, pp. 29–31.

31 Berghaus, *Futurism and Politics*, p. 101.

over many of the Arditi veterans,[32] who became the basis of a Futurist political movement. In 1919 the Arditi veteran and Futurist, Mario Carli, founded the Arditi Association, with *Roma Futurist* as its organ, and the association soon had 10,000 members.[33]

In December 1919, the Futurists revived the "Fasci" or "groups," which had been organized in 1914 and 1915 to campaign for war intervention.[34] From these groups, the Fascists eventually emerged.

FUTURISTS & FASCISTS

The first joint post-war action between Mussolini and Marinetti took place in 1919 when a Socialist Party rally was disrupted in Milan, where the Socialist Leonida Bissolati was trying to advocate a program of Italian renunciation of claims to territories of mainly Italian-speakers under foreign sovereignty. Jensen states that this was "the first planned political violence in post-war Italy."[35]

That year Mussolini founded his own Fasci di Combattimento in Milan with the support of Marinetti and the poet Giuseppe Ungaretti. The Futurists and the Arditi comprised the core of the Fascist leadership. The first Fascist manifesto was based on that of Marinetti's Futurist party.

In April, against the wishes of Mussolini who thought the action premature, Marinetti led Fascists, Futurists, and Arditi against a mass Socialist Party demonstration. Marinetti waded in with his fists, but intervened to save a socialist from being severely beaten by Arditi. (To place the

---

[32] Jensen, "Futurism and Fascism," p. 38.

[33] Jensen, "Futurism and Fascism," p. 38.

[34] The Leagues (Fascio) of Revolutionary Action, revolutionary syndicalists who agitated for Italian entry into the war. Their appeal for war as a revolutionary cause, "To the Workers of Italy," October 10, 1914, can be read in Griffin, *Fascism*, pp. 24–25.

[35] Jensen, "Futurism and Fascism," p. 38.

post-war situation in perspective, the Socialists had regularly beaten, abused, and even killed returning war veterans.) The Fascists and Futurists then proceeded to the offices of the Socialist Party paper *Avanti!*, which they sacked and burned.[36]

Marinetti stood as a Fascist candidate in the 1919 elections in Milan and persuaded Arturo Toscanini to do so. The result was poor.[37]

While the foundation of the Fascist party had been the Futurist-led Arditi veterans, the extreme rejection of tradition by the Futurists make for an uneasy alliance with the Fascists, despite their doctrinal foundation of dialectical synthesis. It is clear that Marinetti did not believe in any such synthesis, which he would surely have regarded as a compromise with "pastism."

When the Fascist Congress of 1920 refused to support the Futurist demand to exile the King and the Pope, Marinetti and other Futurists resigned from the Fascist party. Marinetti held that the Fascist party was compromising with conservatism and the bourgeoisie. He was also critical of the Fascist concentration on anti-socialist agitation and its opposition to strikes.

Certain Futurist factions realigned themselves specifically with the extreme Left. In 1922, there were several Futurist exhibitions and performances in Turin organized by the Communist cultural association, Proletkult, which also arranged a lecture by Marinetti to explain the doctrine of Futurism. However, despite the pro-Futurist sentiments of Soviet education commissar Anatoly Lunacharsky, the Len-

---

[36] Jensen, "Futurism and Fascism," p. 39. The riot became known as the "Battle of Via Mercanti."

[37] Alastair Hamilton, *The Appeal of Fascism: A Study of Intellectuals and Fascism, 1919–1945* (New York: The Macmillan Company, 1971), p. 21.

inists soon rejected Futurism, and Futurist elements were purged from the Communist Party.[38]

FUTURISM & THE FASCIST REGIME

When the Fascists assumed power in 1922, Marinetti, like D'Annunzio, was critically supportive of the regime. Marinetti considered: "The coming to power of Fascism represent[s] the realization of the minimum Futurist program."[39] He alluded to the role Futurists played in founding the Arditi veterans associations and in being among the first members of the *Fasci di combattimento.*

Of Mussolini the statesman, Marinetti wrote: "Prophets and harbingers of the great Italy of today, we Futurists are happy to salute in the Prime Minister, not yet 40, a marvelous Futurist temperament."

In 1923, Marinetti began a rapprochement with the Fascists, Mussolini now having assumed the Premiership of Italy. On May 1, 1923, Marinetti's manifesto "Italian Empire" reminded Mussolini of the Futurist agitation for Italy's imperial revival, and urged Mussolini to reject any alliance with conservatives, monarchists, clerics, or socialists.[40]

That year he also presented to Mussolini his manifesto "The Artistic Rights Promoted by Italian Futurists."[41] Here he rejected the Bolshevik alignment of the Futurists in the USSR. He pointed to the Futurist sentiments that had been expressed by Mussolini in speeches, alluding to Fascism being a "government of speed, curtailing everything that represents stagnation in the national life." Under Mussoli-

---

[38] Berghaus, *Futurism and Politics,* p. 209.

[39] Marinetti, "Benito Mussolini," appendix to Antonio Beltramelli, *L'uomo nuovo* (Milan: Monadori, 1923), in Griffin, *Fascism,* p. 45.

[40] Berghaus, *Futurism and Politics,* pp. 219–20.

[41] Berghaus, *Futurism and Politics,* pp. 194–96.

ni's leadership, writes Marinetti:

> Fascism has rejuvenated Italy. It is now his duty to help us overhaul the artistic establishment. . . . The political revolution must sustain the artistic revolutions Marinetti was among the Congress of Fascist Intellectuals who in 1923 approved the measures taken by the regime to restore order by curtailing certain constitutional liberties amidst increasing chaos caused by both out-of-control radical Fascist *squadristi* and anti-Fascists.

At the 1924 Futurist Congress, the delegates upheld Marinetti's declaration:

> The Italian Futurists . . . more than ever devoted to ideas and art, far removed from politics, say to their old comrade Benito Mussolini: "Free yourself from parliament with one necessary and violent stroke. Restore to Fascism and Italy the marvelous, disinterested, bold, anti-socialist, anti-clerical, anti-monarchical *diciannovista* spirit . . . Refuse to let [monarchy] suffocate the greatest, most brilliant and just Italy of tomorrow. . . . Quell the clerical opposition . . . with a steely and dynamic aristocracy of thought . . .[42]

In 1929, Marinetti accepted election to the Italian Academy, considering it important that "Futurism be represented." He was also elected secretary of the Fascist Writer's Union and as such was the official representative for Fascist culture.[43] Futurism became a part of Fascist cultural exhibitions and was utilized in the propaganda art of the

---

[42] Hamilton, *The Appeal of Fascism*, pp. 51–52.

[43] Hamilton, *The Appeal of Fascism*, p. 65.

regime. During the 1930s in particular, Fascist cultural expression drifted away from tradition and towards Futurism, with the Fascist emphasis on technology and modernization. Mussolini had already in 1926 defined the creation of a "Fascist art" that would be based on a synthesis culturally as it was politically: "traditionalistic and at the same time modern."[44] However, Futurism never became the official "state art" of the Fascist regime. Roger Griffin states: "In stark contrast to the Third Reich, Fascist Italy accommodated various shades of modernism (including the international movement, Futurism, and abstraction) alongside neo-classical or openly anti-modernist ones."[45]

Of the modernist movements other than Futurism, Novecento (Twentieth Century) seems to have been the most significant. Novecento celebrated the dynamism of modern city life and developed a neo-classical architecture.[46] On the other side, there were those prominent Fascists who pursued a more familiar Rightist position in opposing aesthetic modernism as internationalistic, bastardized, foreign, "a racket manipulated by Jewish bankers, pederasts, war-profiteers, brothel keepers," which if adopted would corrupt the Italian race—as Mino Maccari, editor of *Il Selvaggio*, put it, with a specific reference to

---

[44] Mussolini, speech at the opening of the Novecento Italiano exhibition, Milan, 1926, quoted in Simonetta Falasca-Zamponi, *Fascist Spectacle: The Aesthetics of Power in Mussolini's Italy* (Berkeley: University of California Press, 1997), p. 15.

Margherita Sarfatti, a Jewess, was a luminary in the Novecento movement. A writer and art critic, she was also Mussolini's first biographer and worked for Mussolini's newspaper *Il Popolo d'Italia*. She was also Mussolini's mistress. The movement vied with the Futurists to become the state's official "Fascist Art," but Mussolini left the issue open.

[45] Griffin, *Fascism*, p. 60.

[46] Griffin, *Fascism*, p. 61.

Novecento.[47]

Nonetheless, Futurism retained its position among the other aesthetic schools, modernist and traditional, and Marinetti himself remained faithful to Mussolini to the bitter end.

In 1943, with the Allies invading Italy, the Fascist Grand Council deposed Mussolini and surrendered to the occupation forces. The Fascist faithful established a last stand in the north named the Italian Social Republic, or the Republic of Salò.

With a new idealism, even former Communist[48] and liberal leaders were drawn to the Republic. The Manifesto of Verona was drafted, restoring various liberties, and championing labor against plutocracy within the vision of a united Europe.[49]

Marinetti continued to be honored by the Social Republic. He died in 1944.

---

[47] Mino Maccari, *Il Selvaggio,* no. 2, 1927, in Griffin, *Fascism,* p. 60.

[48] Ex-Communist ideologue Nicola Bombacci was a prominent supporter of the Social Republic and co-authored the new program of the Fascist Republican Party (Griffin, *Fascism,* p. 86).

[49] Griffin, *Fascism,* pp. 86–87.

CHAPTER 5

W. B. YEATS

WILLIAM BUTLER YEATS (1865–1939), the Irish poet, leader of the Irish literary renaissance, and winner of the Nobel Prize in Literature in 1923, was among the militants in what Julius Evola called "the revolt against the modern world."[1]

The rise of industrialism and capitalism during the nineteenth century brought with it social dislocation, the rise of commercial interests, and the creation of an urban proletariat on the ruins of rural life. Smashed asunder were the traditional organic bonds of family and village, rootedness to the earth through generations of one's forebears and offspring, and attunement to the cycles of nature. With the ascendancy of materialism came the economic doctrines of free market capitalism and Marxism and the new belief in rationalism and science over faith, the mysteries of the cosmos, and the traditional religions. The forces of money had defeated everything of the spirit. As Oswald Spengler explained in *Decline of the West*, Western Civilization had entered its end phase.[2] Such forces had been let loose as long ago as the English Revolution of Cromwell and again by the French Revolution.

There was, however, a reaction to this predicament. The old conservatives had not been up to the task. The spiritual and cultural reaction came from the artists, po-

---

[1] Julius Evola, *Revolt Against the Modern World*, trans. Guido Stucco (Rochester, Ver.: Inner Traditions, 1995).

[2] Oswald Spengler, *The Decline of the West*, 2 vols., trans. Charles Francis Atkinson (London: George Allen and Unwin, 1971).

ets, and writers who reach beyond the material and draw their inspiration from the wellsprings of what C. G. Jung identified as the collective unconscious. This reaction included not only the political and the cultural but also a spiritual revival expressed in an interest in the metaphysical.

Despite his English and Protestant background, Yeats was involved in the Young Ireland movement, much of his poetry celebrating the Irish rebellion and its heroes.[3]

Yeats wrote of his return to England in 1887 and how the drab modernity of London impressed upon his aesthetic sense the nature of the crisis that was unfolding for civilization:

> I could not understand where the charm had gone that I had felt, when as a school-boy of twelve or thirteen, I had played among the unfinished houses, once leaving the marks of my two hands, blacked by a fall among some paint, upon a white balustrade. Sometimes I thought it was because these were real houses, while my play had been among toy-houses some day to be inhabited by imaginary people full of the happiness that one can see in picture books. I was in all things Pre-Raphaelite.
>
> . . . I remember feeling disappointed because the co-operative stores, with their little seventeenth century panes, were so like any common shop; and because the public house, called "The Tabard" after Chaucer's Inn, was so plainly a common public house; and because the great sign of a trumpeter designed by Rooke, the Pre-Raphaelite artist, had been freshened by some inferior hand.[4]

---

3 W. B. Yeats, "Easter, 1916."

4 W. B. Yeats, *Four Years, 1887–1891* (Dublin: The Cuala

As a youngster, Yeats had been introduced by his father John, himself a Pre-Raphaelite artist, to the paintings of the Pre-Raphaelite school, whose romantic imagery then stood as a rebellion against the encroachments of modernism and industrialism. Having lived in England as a child twenty years before, Yeats was now struck by how much had radically changed under the impress of "progress." The modern era had even impacted upon the aesthetic of Yeats' own family, writing of how his father now made his living, and also alluding to the changes being wrought by modernism in art:

> It was a perpetual bewilderment that my father, who had begun life as a Pre-Raphaelite painter, now painted portraits of the first comer, children selling newspapers, or a consumptive girl with a basket of fish upon her head, and that when, moved perhaps by memory of his youth, he chose some theme from poetic tradition, he would soon weary and leave it unfinished. I had seen the change coming bit by bit and its defence elaborated by young men fresh from the Paris art-schools. "We must paint what is in front of us," or "A man must be of his own time," they would say, and if I spoke of Blake or Rossetti they would point out his bad drawing and tell me to admire Carolus-Duran and Bastien-Lepage. Then, too, they were very ignorant men; they read nothing, for nothing mattered but "Knowing how to paint," being in reaction against a generation that seemed to have wasted its time upon so many things.[5]

Yeats at that time could still see promise in the youth,

Press, 1921), ch. 1.

[5] Yeats, *Four Years,* ch. 2.

in a romantic rebellion against modernism, difficult for us to understand now, when the youthful "rebellion" (*sic*) of our own time transpired to be the highly bogus hippies and "New Left," and then the present generation of consumers. But at that time Yeats could still say of the youth:

> I thought myself alone in hating these young men,[6] now indeed getting towards middle life, their contempt for the past, their monopoly of the future, but in a few months I was to discover others of my own age, who thought as I did, for it is not true that youth looks before it with the mechanical gaze of a well-drilled soldier. Its quarrel is not with the past, but with the present, where its elders are so obviously powerful, and no cause seems lost if it seems to threaten that power. Does cultivated youth ever really love the future, where the eye can discover no persecuted Royalty hidden among oak leaves, though from it certainly does come so much proletarian rhetoric?[7]

He had maintained a religious outlook against materialism, rationalism, and the worship of science and "progress":

> I had made a new religion, almost an infallible church, out of poetic tradition: a fardel of stories, and of personages, and of emotions, a bundle of images and of masks passed on from generation to generation by poets & painters with some help from philosophers and theologians. I wished for a world where I could discover this tradition perpetually,

[6] The modernists.

[7] Yeats, *Four Years*, ch. 2.

> and not in pictures and in poems only, but in tiles round the chimney-piece and in the hangings that kept out the draught. I had even created a dogma: "Because those imaginary people are created out of the deepest instinct of man, to be his measure and his norm, whatever I can imagine those mouths speaking may be the nearest I can go to truth." When I listened they seemed always to speak of one thing only: they, their loves, every incident of their lives, were steeped in the supernatural.[8]

It was against this background of resistance to the modern world that Yeats, having already been acquainted with Theosophy in Dublin, sought out Helena Blavatsky who had recently come to England, a woman with whom he was impressed as having a vast knowledge of what is called the "Ageless Wisdom" or "Perennial Tradition."[9]

For Blavatsky's "hidden masters"[10] Yeats provides a relatively plausible explanation, and one that might be as readily accepted by adherents to the theory of the Collective Unconscious and archetypes postulated by Jung:

---

[8] Yeats, *Four Years*, ch. 2. However, it might be asked whether the enormous interest in wizardry and fantasy, and in new forms of the heroic epic, in film and literature among present-day youngsters (J. R. R. Tolkien, Harry Potter, and the like) is an embryonic reaction against the modern world. Does this express a yearning for the return of something deeper, religion and the mystical having been driven from life by science, technology, and the shopping mall?

[9] Yeats, *Four Years*, ch. 17.

[10] "Hidden Masters," supposedly controllers of the world in some remote region such as Tibet, manifesting their desires to lesser mortals through their chosen vehicles, have been in vogue since Blavatsky's day, and often provide the legitimacy for claims to occult leadership.

> I thought that her masters were imaginary forms created by suggestion, but whether that suggestion came from Madame Blavatsky's own mind or from some mind, perhaps at a great distance, I did not know; and I believed that these forms could pass from Madame Blavatsky's mind to the minds of others, and even acquire external reality, and that it was even possible that they talked and wrote. They were born in the imagination, where Blake had declared that all men live after death, and where "every man is king or priest in his own house."[11]

It was around this time that Yeats happened to meet MacGregor Mathers, an author and a student of the occult, at the British Museum Reading Room, and to begin studies of occultism under his guidance, writing: "and it was through him mainly that I began certain studies and experiences that were to convince me that images well up before the mind's eye from a deeper source than conscious or subconscious memory."[12]

---

[11] Yeats, *Four Years,* ch. 18. The notion of "thought forms" being able to take on an independent existence should not perhaps be automatically dismissed as nonsense. The present-day scientist Rupert Sheldrake, a biologist of repute, has devoted much research into the possibility of what he calls the "morphic field" and "morphic resonance," which is analogous to what mystics call the "astral plane," where thought forms might take tangible shape. Rupert Sheldrake Website: http://www.sheldrake.org/homepage.html

A fascinating example of what Yeats seems to be hypothesizing is the famous Philip Experiment in Toronto in 1972, in which a group "thought form" was created that took on a personality and even a history and name of its own.

[12] Yeats, *Four Years,* ch. 19. Here again one could have recourse to Jung's concept of the Collective Unconscious, alt-

Mathers was a co-founder and head of the Hermetic Order of the Golden Dawn, the primary organization around which there was an occult revival. Yeats was initiated in 1890, and was within a few years an Adept in its governing body, the "Second Order."[13]

For Yeats the mystical was the basis of both his poetry and his political ideas. He was particularly interested in the Irish mystical tradition and folklore. He saw the peasantry and rural values as being necessary to revive against the onslaught of materialism. He aimed to found an Irish Hermetic Order, an "Order of Celtic Mysteries," as he aimed to call it, replacing the alien Egyptian gods of Golden Dawn ritual with the Irish gods and heroes.[14]

Yeats saw the mythic and spiritual as the basis of a culture, providing the underlying unity for all cultural manifestations, a "unity of being," where, writing in reference to Byzantine culture: "[The] religious, aesthetic, and practical life were one . . . the painter, the mosaic worker, the worker in gold and silver, the illuminator of sacred books were absorbed in the subject matter, and that of the vision of a whole people."[15]

ARCHETYPES & THE MULTITUDE

Yeats held that symbols had an autonomous power of their own in the unconscious. It was these symbols, agelong inherited memories, upon which the artist and the

---

hough Yeats seems to have developed an analogous theory on his own account.

[13] Ellic Howe, *The Magicians of the Golden Dawn* (Northamptonshire: The Aquarian Press, 1985), pp. 100–102.

[14] Terence Brown, *The Life of W. B. Yeats: A Critical Biography* (Oxford: Blackwell, 2001), p. 119.

[15] Alexander Norman Jeffares, *A New Commentary on the Poems of W. B. Yeats* (Stanford, Cal.: Stanford University Press, 1984), p. 212, citing: "A Vision: Notes on Sailing to Byzantium."

poet drew as the source of creativity.

To Yeats, "individuality is not as important as our age has imagined."[16] The *daimons*[17] of the ancient memories acted upon the individual, and one's creativity was an expression of these forces. These symbols and images could be brought to consciousness and expressed artistically via magic and ritual; hence Yeats' involvement in metaphysical societies such as the Golden Dawn and Theosophy. Additionally, the "occult" provided a literally hidden culture that was above and beyond the crassness of democracy, of the herd, and of material existence, hence its being termed the "Royal Art," where again, as in traditional societies over the course of millennia, a priestly caste, at the apex of a hierarchical society, served as the nexus between the terrestrial and the divine, serving as that axis around which High Culture revolves.[18]

---

[16] Brown, *The Life of W. B. Yeats*, p. 117.

[17] Greek, one's higher intuitive, creative faculties.

[18] The pre-eminent nineteenth-century historian of the occult, Eliphas Lévi (Alphonse Louis Constant) referred to the aristocratic tradition of the occult as elevating the adept to the "rank of kings, because magical initiation constitutes a true royalty . . . characterized by all Adepts as the Royal Art." See Eliphas Lévi, *The History of Magic*, trans. A. E. Waite (London: Rider, 1982), p. 5. Like Evola and René Guénon, Lévi, a former socialist agitator and Freemason of the Rose-Cross Degree, also warned of an anti-tradition that included Freemasonry and that was behind the French Revolution: "The anarchists have resumed the rule, square, and mallet, writing upon them the word Liberty, Equality, Fraternity—Liberty, that is to say, for all lusts, Equality in degradation, and Fraternity in the work of destruction. Such are the men whom the Church has condemned justly and will condemn for ever" (p. 287). See also: Book 6, chapter 4: "The French Revolution." It is of interest that the French Revolutionary slogan "Liberty, Equality, Fraternity," also happens to be the slogan of the Grand Orient of

Yeats' poetry was intended as an expression of these symbols of the unconscious and the archetypal. This resurgence of these age-long memories required a "revolt of soul against intellect now beginning in the world."[19] What is here called "intellect" was the advance of rationalism, scientism, and Enlightenment doctrines that had destroyed man's nexus with the divine embodied in traditions and hierarchical social orders, and which has repressed man's spiritual nature in favor of the crassly material. Spengler referred to the same cultural predicament when he wrote of the conflict in the final stages of a civilization between "blood" and "money," the "intellect" being the superficial that is at the service of money, "blood" being a metaphor for the traditional (i.e., the organic).[20]

Yeats, like D. H. Lawrence, Ezra Pound, *et al.*, was particularly concerned that commercialism would mean the pushing down of cultural values in the pursuit of profit rather than artistic excellence. Hence, he called for a revival of aristocratic values. He lamented that "the mere multitude is everywhere with its empty photographic eyes. A declaration of war on the masses by higher men is called for. Everywhere the mediocre are coming in order to make themselves master."[21]

His appeal was to the artist and to the individual of taste and culture, for, as Nietzsche had pointed out, culture is the faculty that distinguishes the human from other organisms. In this spirit, Yeats applauded Nietzsche's philosophy as "a counteractive to the spread of

---

France.

[19] W. B. Yeats, "Letter to John O'Leary," 1892.

[20] "Money is overthrown and abolished only by blood" (Oswald Spengler, *The Decline of the West*, vol. 2, p. 507).

[21] W. B. Yeats, *On the Boiler* (Dublin: The Cuala Press, 1938), p. 25.

democratic vulgarity."[22]

This suspicion of democratic vulgarity, specifically what appears to be a condemnation of the democratization of literature known as the "news media," was poetically expressed, for example, in 1921 in "The Leaders of the Crowd":

> They must to keep their certainty accuse
> All that are different of a base intent;
> Pull down established honour; hawk for news
> Whatever their loose phantasy invent . . . [23]

Here Yeats is condemning the leveling effects of the democratic media, pandering to the lowest denominator for the sake of maximum profit via the largest market, part of a general commodification of culture, which was why Yeats, like Lawrence, Wyndham Lewis, Pound, *et al.*, deplored the democratization process.

Yeats' keen sense of historical context is reflected in "The Curse of Cromwell." Here he identifies the English Revolution as the inauguration of the stage of "Money over Blood," in Spenglerian terms: the victory of the merchant class over the traditional order, which was to be reenacted in the French Revolution.[24] The Bolshevik Revolution was born of the same spirit of materialism against spirit and culture. All three revolutions were carried out in the name of "the people" against the traditional rulers, only to create a greater tyranny in the service of money.

---

[22] John Carey, *The Intellectuals and the Masses: Pride and Prejudice Among the Literary Intelligentsia, 1880–1939* (London: Faber & Faber, 1992), p. 25.

[23] W. B. Yeats, *Michael Robartes and the Dancer*, "The Leaders of the Crowd" (Dublin: The Cuala Press, 1921).

[24] Spengler, *The Decline of the West*, vol. 2, p. 507.

Spengler had written in *The Decline of the West*: "Practical communism with its 'class-war' . . . is nothing but the trusty henchman of big Capital, which knows perfectly well how to make use of it."[25] "In this sense, the interest-politics of the workers' movements also belong to it [capitalism], in that their object is not to overcome the money-values, but to possess them."[26]

Cromwell's English revolution has had lasting consequences for the entire West. The dominion of money over culture and tradition that Cromwell inaugurated has never been overcome. America was founded on the same Puritan money ethics and continues to spread that spirit over the farthest reaches of the world.

Cromwell's "murderous crew" have brought forth "money's rant" on the blood of what is noble:

> You ask what I have found and far and wide I go,
> Nothing but Cromwell's house and Cromwell's murderous crew,
> The lovers and the dancers are beaten into the clay,
> And the tall men and the swordsmen and the horsemen, where are they?
> And there is an old beggar wandering in his pride
> His fathers served their fathers before Christ was crucified
> *O what of that, O what of that?*
> *What is there left to say?*

The specter of Puritanism has haunted the entire world ever since, "far and wide." Nobility of character, regardless of "class"—itself a vulgarization of the traditional *castes*—was destroyed by the inauguration in the West of the reign of money by Cromwell, and one that was not

[25] Spengler, *The Decline of the West*, vol. 2, p. 506, n1.
[26] Spengler, *The Decline of the West*, vol. 2, p. 506, n2.

overcome, but rather adopted by its supposed "enemy," socialism, as Spengler was to point out. Yeats, as "The Curse of Cromwell" shows, was one of the few to realize the full depth and lasting significance of Puritanism under whatever name it might appear.

Spengler pointed out the nature of Puritanism in the same spirit as Yeats, referring to Puritanism, not only in the West, but its analogous manifestations in other cultures in their cycle of decay, which "lacks the smile that had illuminated the religion of the Spring . . .[27] the moments of profound joy in life, the humour of life."[28] Yeats discerned the same: "The lovers and the dancers are beaten into the clay/And the tall men and the swordsmen and the horsemen, where are they?"

Gone are those of noble tradition, those who served as part of a long heritage, "the tall men"; the old gaiety of the peasant village, the squire's hall, and aristocrat's manor has been beaten down:

All neighbourly content and easy talk are gone,
But there's no good complaining, for money's rant is on.

The artists, once patronized by the aristocracy, must now prostitute their art for the sake of money on the mass market, as scriptwriters, and "public entertainers" to sell a product. All individuals are now producers and consumers, including the artist producing for a consumer market.

And we and all the Muses are things of no account.

Yeats considered himself heir to a tradition that has

---

[27] Spengler referred to the "analogous historical epochs" of Civilizations in terms of the Seasons, to emphasize the organic nature of his cyclic historical paradigm.

[28] Spengler, *The Decline of the West*, vol. 2, p. 302.

been repressed by democratic vulgarity, and he lived in service to that tradition, now virtually driven to the catacombs under the dead weight of "mass culture," which is nothing more than consumerism posturing as "art," "literature," and "music" manufactured according to market demands. He and a few others of the same temperament lived in the service of High Culture as contemporary troubadours "against the modern world" to uplift the spirits of the remnant who have managed to maintain their nobility in the face of the crass:

> That the swordsmen and the ladies can still keep company;
> Can pay the poet for a verse and hear the fiddle sound,
> That I am still their servant though all are underground.

Order from Chaos

One product of democracy and capitalism that Yeats feared was the proliferation of those he regarded as inferior people. Yeats advocated planned human upbreeding and joined the Eugenics Society at a time when eugenics was a widely held belief among the intelligentsia. As with his political and cultural views, however, his outlook on eugenics had a mystical basis, relating reincarnation to the race soul. In his 1938 poem "Under Ben Bulben," Yeats calls in eugenic terms for Irish poets to sing of "whatever is well made," and "scorn the sort now growing up," "all out of shape from toe to top." In this poem, there is a mixture of the mythic, reincarnation, the race soul, and eugenics. There is an immortality of the soul that parts one in death only briefly from the world:

> Many times man lives and dies
> Between his two eternities

That of race and that of soul
And ancient Ireland knew it all.[29]

The eugenic and the divine combine within the artist:

Poet and sculptor do the work
Nor let the modish painter shirk
What his great forefathers did,
Bring the soul of man to God,
Make him fill the cradles right.

However, in the modern age, "The greater dream had gone. Confusion fell upon our thought." It is the duty of the cultural-bearing stratum to set the culture anew by remembering what had once been:

Irish poets learn your trade
Sing whatever is well made,
Scorn the sort now growing up
All out of shape from toe to top,
Their unremembering hearts and heads
Base-born products of base beds.

Yeats' antidote to the modern era of decline is to return to the traditional order of peasant, squire, monk, and aristocrat:

Sing the peasantry, and then
Hard-riding country gentlemen,
The holiness of monks, and after
Porter-drinkers' randy laughter;
Sing the lords and ladies gay
That were beaten into the clay

---

[29] W. B. Yeats, "Under Ben Bulben," 1938.

Through seven heroic centuries;
Cast your mind on other days
That we in coming days may be
Still the indomitable Irishry.

Returning to eugenics, Yeats had *On the Boiler* published the same year, where he endorsed the psychometric studies that showed intelligence to be inherited, and expressed concern at the proliferation of the unintelligent.[30]

In "The Old Stone Cross," Yeats compares the modern era to traditional society:

A statesman is an easy man,
He tells his lies by rote;
A journalist makes up his lies
And takes you by the throat;
So stay at home and drink your beer
And let the neighbours vote
Said the man in the golden breastplate
Under the old stone Cross

Because this age and the next
Engender in the ditch . . .[31]

The democratic farce, with its politicians, newspapermen, and voting masses, is not worthy of attention. The modern cycle is also dealt with in "The Statesman's Holiday," where:

I lived among great houses,
Riches drove out rank,

---

30 W. B. Yeats, *On the Boiler* (Dublin: The Cuala Press, 1938).
31 W. B. Yeats, "The Old Stone Cross," 1938.

Base drove out the better blood,
And mind and body shrank.[32]

The aristocracy of old, the noble lineage of blood, of familial descent, has been replaced by the new rich, the merchants, our new rulers are those who measure all things by profit.

FALL & RISE

In 1921, the year prior to Mussolini's assumption to power, Yeats had prophesied in "The Second Coming" the approach of a figure from out of the democratic chaos, a "rough beast" who would settle matters amidst a world where, when "things fall apart, the centre cannot hold."

The theme is reminiscent of Spengler's account of the return of "Caesarism" at the end of Civilization, in a type of last hurrah, or final dying breath when the Civilization briefly reasserts itself against money and returns to its founding values.[33] In the Spenglerian cyclic paradigm, there is not only a decline and fall of a civilization but an interregnum where the "new Caesar" emerges from the decadent epoch to inaugurate a revitalization of the civilization. Yeats' poem opens with an allusion to the "turning" of the historic cycles:

Turning and turning in the widening gyre
The falcon cannot hear the falconer:
Things fall apart; the centre cannot hold;[34]

---

[32] W. B. Yeats, "The Statesman's Holiday," 1938.

[33] "The coming of Caesarism breaks the dictature of money and its political weapon democracy" (Spengler, *The Decline of the West*, vol. 2, p. 506).

[34] W. B. Yeats, "The Second Coming," 1921.

Here Yeats is portraying history as a cycle reminiscent of a wheel, where the axis around which the civilization revolves is that of Tradition, but as the civilization advances along the path of cyclic decay, it begins to fall asunder as the axis of Tradition is no longer strong enough to hold the structure of civilization together. "The falcon cannot hear the falconer": "modern" man in the last phase of every civilization no longer hears the call of his Tradition, or metaphorically, his "blood." He is detached and loses the anchorage of the axis of Tradition. Consequently everything falls apart: the civilization dies, and its light is extinguished, existing perhaps only in the form of ruins of once great monuments, of the Colosseum and the pyramids. Although Yeats had worked out his theory of history prior to reading Spengler, he found the coincidence between his views and those expressed in *The Decline of the West*, "too great for coincidence,"[35] or perhaps what one might call in Jungian terms synchronistic.

> Mere anarchy is loosed upon the world,
> The blood-dimmed tide is loosed, and everywhere
> The ceremony of innocence is drowned;
> The best lack all conviction, while the worst
> Are full of passionate intensity.

One can read in the above what appears to be then the growing tide of Bolshevik revolution amidst the loss of tradition, having described Marxism as "the super-head of materialism and leading to inevitable murder."[36] The answer is the rise of a strong leader who will get civilization back on course, the "new Caesar" that Spengler later

---

[35] W. B. Yeats, *A Vision* (New York: Macmillan, 1961), p. 261.

[36] Allen Wade, ed., *The Letters of W. B. Yeats* (London: Rupert Hart-Davis, 1954), p. 656.

saw in the possibility of Mussolini.

> Surely some revelation is at hand;
> Surely the Second Coming is at hand.[37]

Like Spengler, Yeats saw hope in Fascist Italy: "The Ireland that reacts from the present disorder is turning its eyes towards individualist Italy." In particular, he admired the educational reforms and cyclic historical doctrine of Italian Fascist philosopher and Minister of Education, Giovanni Gentile, stating in 1925 before the Irish Senate, of which he was a member, that Irish teachers should study the methods that Gentile had enacted in Italian schools, "so to correlate all subjects of study."[38] The following year Senator Yeats[39] stated that the Italian educational system was "adapted to an agricultural nation" which was applicable also to Ireland, "a system of education that will not turn out clerks only, but will turn out efficient men and women, who can manage to do all the work of the nation."[40]

In 1933, the year after Éamon de Valera came to power, Yeats sought to formulate a doctrine for Ireland that would be a form of "Fascism modified by religion."[41] History consisted broadly of "the rule of the many followed by the rule of the few," again reminiscent of Spengler's idea of a "new Caesarism" that follows on the rule of plutocracy at the end phase of a civilization. For Yeats, the

---

[37] Yeats, "The Second Coming."

[38] D. R. Pearse, ed., *The Senate Speeches of W. B. Yeats* (London: Faber & Faber, 1961), p. 173.

[39] Yeats had been appointed to the first Irish Senate in 1922 and was reappointed in 1925.

[40] *The Senate Speeches of W. B. Yeats,* p. 111.

[41] *The Letters of W. B. Yeats,* p. 808.

rule of the few meant a return to some form of aristocracy.[42]

That year, 1933, Yeats met General Eoin O'Duffy, leader of the Irish Blueshirts, whom Yeats thought might be capable of overthrowing de Valera and instituting a sound government. O'Duffy, a hero of the Irish revolt and Michael Collins' principal aide, created a mass movement, one of the many "corporatist" movements that were sprouting up all over Europe and further afield in the midst of the Depression, and Eire was almost brought to civil war between his "Blueshirts" and the IRA.[43] Yeats approvingly regarded the Blueshirts as part of a worldwide movement of "fascism"[44] and wrote three marching songs for them. These sang of the heroes of Ireland, and of the need for a renewed social order:

> When nations are empty up there at the top,
> When order has weakened and faction is strong,
> Time for us to pick out a good tune,
> Take to the roads and go marching along . . .

However, Yeats, like Lewis, Evola, and others, was suspicious of any movement that appealed to the masses, and of what he saw as the demagoguery of the Fascist leaders in appealing to those masses. This was regardless of the fact that the masses were being won over to national ideals and away from the internationalism of the Communists.

Even Spengler expressed reservations about Fascism because of its nature as a mass movement, writing that:

---

[42] *The Letters of W. B. Yeats,* p. 813.

[43] Maurice Manning, *The Blueshirts* (London: Gill and Macmillan, 1970).

[44] Manning, *The Blueshirts,* p. 232.

> Mussolini's creative idea was grand, and it has had an international effect: it revealed a possible form for the combating of Bolshevism. But this form arose out of imitating the enemy and is therefore full of dangers: revolution from below . . .[45]

Yeats, like other members of the literati who were suspicious of mass movements of any form, had the luxury of not subjecting his ideals to the sobering necessities of a practical political struggle to save civilization from communism and capitalism, which is what O'Duffy and others around the world were then trying to accomplish.

But it is not the role of the troubadour to carry out political campaigns, but to maintain the remnants of High Culture amidst the vulgarity of what the Hindus call the Kali Yuga. And in this task, Yeats never wavered.

---

[45] Oswald Spengler, *The Hour of Decision*, Part One: *Germany and World-Historical Evolution*, trans. Charles Francis Atkinson (New York: Knopf, 1963), pp. 186–87. However Spengler also believed that Fascism might transform into something else prefiguring a "new Caesarism" (p. 230).

CHAPTER 6

KNUT HAMSUN

KNUT HAMSUN, 1859–1952, has had a decisive impact on the course of twentieth-century literature, both in Europe and America, yet for decades he was little discussed let alone honored even in his native Norway.

Ernest Hemingway tried to emulate him, as did Henry Miller, who called Hamsun "the Dickens of my generation." Thomas Mann wrote, "never has the Nobel Prize been awarded to one so worthy of it." Hermann Hesse called Hamsun his favorite author. Admired by H. G. Wells, Franz Kafka, and Bertolt Brecht,[1] Hamsun always enjoyed a great following not only in Germany but particularly in Russia, where he was lauded especially by Maxim Gorky. Despite his politics, Hamsun continued to be published in the USSR, influencing such Bolshevik luminaries as Aleksandra Kollontai and Ilya Ehrenburg.[2]

ORIGINS

Hamsun was born Knud Pedersen to an impoverished peasant family of seven children on August 4, 1859. His father was a farmer and a tailor; his mother was descended from Viking nobility. Hamsun had a hard upbringing on his uncle's farm, where he was sent when he was nine. But his uncle also ran the local library, which gave him the chance to begin his self-education.[3]

He left his uncle's farm in 1873, and over the next few

---

[1] Robert Ferguson, *Enigma: The Life of Knut Hamsun* (London: Hutchinson, 1987), p. 300.

[2] Ferguson, *Enigma*, p. 301.

[3] Ferguson, *Enigma*, p. 13.

years worked at a variety of jobs—laboring, teaching, and doing clerical work—as he journeyed widely.[4]

AMERICA

At 18 Hamsun published his first novel called *The Enigmatic One* (1877), a love story. He then paid for the publication of another novel *Bjørger* (1878). But acknowledgment as a writer was a decade away, as there was then little interest in his peasant tales.

In 1882 Hamsun traveled to the United States, joining the great Norwegian emigration to that country. Between numerous jobs he was able to get some newspaper articles published and began a series of lectures on authors among the Norwegian community.[5] From this early start, Hamsun wrote as an observer of life. He was the first to develop the novel based on the psychology of characters. Hamsun wrote of what he saw and felt, particularly identifying with the workers and the tramps. But he was soon disillusioned with America, despite his initial wonder, and he expressed his disgust with American life in articles for Norwegian newspapers[6] upon his return.[7]

In the first sentence of his first article on America[8] Hamsun described the country as "the Millionaires' Republic," a reference to the manner by which elections are

---

[4] Ferguson, *Enigma*, p. 21.

[5] Richard C. Nelson, *Knut Hamsun Remembers America: Essays and Stories, 1885–1949* (Missouri: University of Missouri Press, 2003), pp. 4–5.

[6] Knut Hamsun, "Letters from America," *Knut Hamsun Remembers America*, p. 7.

[7] Ferguson, *Enigma*, p. 68.

[8] Knut Hamsun, "The American Character," *Aftenposten* (Christiania, Norway), January 21, 1885; *Knut Hamsun Remembers America*, pp. 17–18.

based on money,[9] and where the "diseased and degenerate human raw material stream every day from all over the world." Alluding to principles that are today familiarly called "the American Dream," Hamsun states that the immigrant is soon disappointed when "the principles do not deliver what they promise."

He was skeptical about the fetishism of liberty upon which the American ethos is founded, stating that it is in practice not so much a matter of having "liberty" as "taking liberties."[10] The purpose of being American is to fulfill a "carnivorous, satiating existence, with the ability to afford intense sensual pleasures . . ."[11]

What now seems particularly prescient, Hamsun, in criticizing the *"machine lust"* of Americans, alludes with a mixture of amazement and abhorrence to having even eaten an egg "from a Brooklyn *egg factory*" (Hamsun's emphasis),[12] perhaps something that might have seemed pathological for a youthful Scandinavian of country stock.

Hamsun's next article for the *Aftenposten* centered on New York and focused on the vulgarity of American city-dwellers in comparison to those in Europe, e.g., their loudness and their lack of etiquette.[13] "New Yorkers know little about literature or art."[14] The theatre is popular but the "level of dramatic art is so low."[15]

Hamsun's first major literary work came in 1888, when he succeeded in getting a short story, which was to form part of his novel *Hunger*, published in a magazine. The sto-

---

[9] Hamsun, "The American Character," p. 19.

[10] Hamsun, "The American Character," p. 14.

[11] Hamsun, "The American Character," p. 20.

[12] Hamsun, "The American Character," p. 21.

[13] Knut Hamsun, "New York," *Aftenposten*, February 12, 14, 1895; *Knut Hamsun Remembers America*, pp. 28–29.

[14] Hamsun, "New York," p. 29.

[15] Hamsun, "New York," p. 30.

ry gained him access to the literary scene in Copenhagen. Hamsun became a celebrity among younger intellectuals. He was invited to lecture before university audiences.[16]

He was commissioned to write a book on America in 1889, setting aside the completion of *Hunger*. The result was *The Cultural Life of Modern America*,[17] based on his second trip to the US in 1886, which had been prompted by his desire to make a literary mark for himself there.[18]

By 1888 he was so repelled by the US, that he took to wearing a black ribbon in sympathy with four German anarchist immigrants who had been sentenced to death for the 1886 Haymarket bombing in Chicago.[19]

He left a departing message, giving a two-hour lecture on the cultural vacuity of America.[20]

Despite his destitution upon settling in Copenhagen, he wrote to a friend: "How pleased I am with this country. This is Europe, and I am European—thank God!"[21]

It was two lectures on America at the University of Copenhagen that formed the basis of *The Cultural Life of Modern America*. Richard C. Nelson remarks of Hamsun's particular disgust, which might to many readers seem completely relevant to the present time: "In particular he was offended by the exaggerated patriotism of Americans, their continual boasting of themselves as the freest, most advanced, most intelligent people anywhere—boasting from which the foreigner could not escape."[22]

---

[16] Ferguson, *Enigma*, p. 101.

[17] Knut Hamsun, *The Cultural Life of Modern America* (1889), trans. Barbara Gordon Morgridge (Cambridge, Mass.: Harvard University Press, 1969)

[18] *Knut Hamsun Remembers America*, p. 7.

[19] *Knut Hamsun Remembers America*, p. 9.

[20] *Knut Hamsun Remembers America*, p. 9.

[21] *Knut Hamsun Remembers America*, p. 10.

[22] *Knut Hamsun Remembers America*, p. 10.

Hamsun attacked the crass materialism of the US. He despised democracy as a form of despotism, abhorring its leveling nature and mob politics. America is a land where the highest morality is money, where the meaning of art is reduced to its cash value. He also expresses his misgivings about the presence of Africans in the US. The Civil War is described as a war against aristocracy by Northern capitalists. He writes: "Instead of founding an intellectual elite, America has established a mulatto stud farm."

LITERARY EMINENCE

Hamsun resumed writing *Hunger* after his musings on America, publishing the novel in 1890. It has been described as one of the great novels of urban alienation. Like much of his writing, it is partly autobiographical. It centers on a budding young writer trying to fend off poverty, wandering the streets in rags, but in some odd way enjoying the experiences despite the hardship. Through an act of will the character maintains his identity.

This was perhaps the first novel to make the workings of the mind the central theme. It was a genre he was to continue experimenting with over the next ten years. Contra orthodox psychological theories, Hamsun held that a diversity of separate personality types within the individual is a desirable state of being. He wrote of this in regard to his aim for literature: "I will therefore have contradictions in the inner man considered as a quite natural phenomenon, and I dream of a literature with characters in which their very lack of consistency is their basic characteristic.[23]

Hamsun's next great novel was *Mysteries*,[24] virtually a self-portrait. One reviewer described Hamsun as express-

---

[23] Ferguson, *Enigma*, p. 124.

[24] Knut Hamsun, *Mysteries: A Novel* (1892), trans. anonymous (New York: Farrar, Straus and Giroux, 1967).

ing "the wildest paradoxes," a hatred of bourgeois academics and of the masses. The principal character, Nagel, is presented by means of free-flowing, stream of consciousness thought associations.[25]

Here Hamsun identifies himself as "a radical who belongs to no party, but is an individual in the extreme."[26] The book caused an uproar among literary circles, but it sold well.

Having outraged the literary establishment, Hamsun next set about critiquing the younger coterie of writers as arrogant and talentless wastrels, whom he represents in *Shallow Soil*[27] as "a festering sore on the social organism of the Norwegian capital," in the words of Professor Josef Wiehr.[28]

Here Hanka Tidemand, a liberated and modern woman of the type detested by Hamsun, finds her true nature back with her hard-working husband and children, after an affair with an artist. On the verge of divorce, she realizes her mistaken course when she sees her children. Here Hamsun sets out his constant theme of rediscovering one's roots in the simple life, in family, and in children. The well-meaning Mr. Tidemand has his wife Hanka leave after she is seduced by one of the bohemian parasites.

> [Tidemand's] regard for the individual liberty of his wife amounts really to a fault. He fails to see, however, the grave danger which is threatening

---

[25] Ferguson, *Enigma*, p. 133.

[26] Ferguson, *Enigma*, p. 138.

[27] Knut Hamsun, *Shallow Soil* (1893), trans. Carl Christian Hyllested (New York: Charles Scribner's Sons, 1914).

[28] Josef Wiehr, *Knut Hamsun: His Personality and His Outlook upon Life* (Northampton, Mass.: Smith College Studies in Modern Languages, 1922), p. 23.

> Hanka and believes to be promoting her true happiness in according her perfect freedom. His devotion to her never ceases, and when she at last repents, he makes reconciliation easy for her. . . .
>
> Hanka is evidently the product of a misdirected striving for emancipation; she seems to acknowledge no duty except the duty to herself.[29]

The Kareno trilogy of plays (*At the Gates of the Kingdom, Evening Glow,* and *The Game of Life,* 1895–1896) expresses Hamsun's growing anti-democratic sentiment in the character of Ivar Kareno, a young philosopher who states: "I believe in the born leader, the natural despot, not the man who is chosen but the man who elects himself to be ruler over the masses. I believe in and hope for one thing, and that is the return of the great terrorist, the living essence of human power, the Caesar."[30]

By now, Hamsun had become a celebrity, cheered in the streets by crowds although he despised the attention, but several decades away from being honored with a Nobel Prize.

GROWTH OF THE SOIL

Growth of the Soil is a remarkable book for those who have a yearning for the timeless in a world of the superficial and the transient. Published in 1917, it was the work that was cited when Hamsun was awarded the Nobel Prize in Literature in 1920.

This is the world of a rough, coarsely-featured farmer, Isak, and a woman, Inger, who happened to come from across the valley and stay with him to raise a family and help him work the land, raise goats, grow potatoes and

---

[29] Wiehr, *Knut Hamsun,* p. 24.

[30] Ferguson, *Enigma,* p. 164.

corn, milk the cows and goats, make cheese, and subsist at one with nature. Isak and Inger are archetypes of the peasant, the antithesis of the New Yorker and the archetypical "American" described in Hamsun's essays on the US.

The sense of a day-by-day participation in eternity lived by Isak and Inger is captured, juxtaposing their lives with the grain they sow and the earth they till, as part of a single rhythm that has existed for centuries:

> For generations back, into forgotten time, his fathers before him had sowed corn, solemnly, on a still, calm evening, best with a gentle fall of warm and misty rain, soon after the grey goose flight. . . .
>
> Isak walked bareheaded, in Jesu' name, a sower. Like a tree-stump to look at, but in his heart like a child. Every cast was made with care, in a spirit of kindly resignation. Look! The tiny grains that are to take life and to grow, shoot up into ears, and give more corn again; so it is throughout all the earth where corn is sown. Palestine, America, the valleys of Norway itself—a great wide world, and here is Isak, a tiny speck in the midst of it all, a sower. Little showers of corn flung out fanwise from his hand; a kindly clouded sky, with a promise of the faintest little misty rain.[31]

The woman as mother is the highest of peasant values, and indeed of the fulfillment of women, in antithesis to the "liberated woman" that was becoming evident in Hamsun's time as a symptom of a culture's decay, a type already described by Hamsun in *Shallow Soil* and else-

---

[31] Knut Hamsun, *Growth of the Soil* (1920), trans. W. W. Worster (New York: Macmillan, 1980), Book I, ch. 3. http://ebooks.adelaide.edu.au/h/hamsun/knut/h23g/index.html

where.

The rearing of children is the purpose of Being of the wife and mother, as much as that might be sneered at now, but as Spengler noted, there is nothing more important than the continuation of a family lineage, generation after generation, and one might add—interestingly—the same values hold as true for the aristocrat as for the peasant; there is nothing more dreadful than being the last of a family's line. Hence, we see something of this feeling described by Hamsun: "She was in full flower and constantly with child. Isak himself, her lord and master, was earnest and stolid as ever, but he had got on well, and was content. How he had managed to live until Inger came was a mystery . . . now, he had all that a man can think of in his place in the world."[32]

The feeling is described by Oswald Spengler in *The Hour of Decision*:

> A woman of race[33] does not desire to be a "companion" or a "lover," but a *mother*; and not the mother of *one* child, to serve as a toy and a distraction, but of many; the instinct of a strong race speaks in the pride that large families inspire, in the feeling that barrenness is the hardest curse that can befall a woman and through her the race . . .[34]

This is precisely the type of woman that Inger represents:

---

[32] Hamsun, *Growth of the Soil*, ch. 4.

[33] It needs to be pointed out that by "race" Spengler did not a biological, or "Darwinistic" conception, but an instinct. "Race" means "duration of character," including "an urge to permanence." See Oswald Spengler, *The Hour of Decision*, Part One: *Germany and World-Historical Evolution*, trans. Charles Francis Atkinson (New York: Alfred A. Knopf, 1963), p. 220.

[34] Spengler, *The Hour of Decision*, p. 220.

"She was in full flower, and constantly with child . . ." Spengler continues: "A man wants stout sons who will perpetuate his name and his deeds beyond his death into the future and enhance them, just as he has done himself through feeling himself heir to the calling and works of his ancestors."[35]

This organic conception of family, an instinct during the "Spring" and "Summer" epochs of a civilization, becomes atrophied during the "Autumn" and "Winter" epochs, as Spengler aptly terms the morphological phases of a culture; which is of course the situation today, and was becoming apparent during Hamsun's time. The culture-problem addressed by Hamsun in *Shallow Soil*, where the "emancipated woman" leaves her family, is described by Spengler:

> The *meaning* of man and wife, the will to perpetuity, is being lost. People live for themselves alone, not for future generations. The nation as society, once the organic web of *families*, threatens to dissolve, from the city outwards, into a sum of *private atoms*, of which each is intent on extracting from his own and other lives the maximum of amusement—*panem et cicenses*. The women's emancipation of Ibsen's time wanted, not freedom from the husband, but freedom from the child, from the *burden* of children, just as men's emancipation in the same period signified freedom from the *duties* towards family, nation, and State.[36]

Hamsun addressed a matter of land ownership and purchase, as it had been the habit of the tillers to simply stake out a plot of land and work it, without thought as to how

---

[35] Spengler, *The Hour of Decision*, pp. 220–21.
[36] Spengler, *The Hour of Decision*, pp. 221–22.

and where to purchase it. Amidst the cycles of struggle, drought, crop failures, births of children, and crop recovery, and the contentedness of Isak and Inger and their family amidst it all, an official calls upon them one day to enquire as to why Isak never bought the land.

> Buy, what should he buy for? The ground was there, the forest was there; he had cleared and tilled, built up a homestead in the midst of a natural wilderness, winning bread for himself and his, asking nothing of any man, but working, and working alone.[37]

The district sheriff's officer finally calls by, looking at the vast tracts of tilled land, and asking why Isak had never come to him to purchase it. Soon after a bit of verbal sophistry, Isak begins to see how the official must be correct. Asking about "boundaries," Isak had only thought in terms of how far he could see and what he could work. But the State required "definite boundaries," "and the greater the extent, the more you will have to pay." To all of this, Isak could only acknowledge with "Ay."[38]

From there, the simple life of Isak and Inger is confronted with a bureaucratic muddle, with questions on the money-value of the land, its waters, the potential for fishing, and the possibility of ores and metals.

Then civilization reaches Isak and Inger in the form of the telegraph (which becomes a metaphor for "civilization") which is to go through his land, and for which he would be paid to maintain the lines.[39] Furthermore, copper is discovered in the hills Isak owns.[40] But despite the mon-

---

[37] Hamsun, *Growth of the Soil*, ch. 5.

[38] Hamsun, *Growth of the Soil*, ch. 5.

[39] Hamsun, *Growth of the Soil*, ch. 9.

[40] Hamsun, *Growth of the Soil*, ch. 10.

ey that now comes to Isak, he remains always a peasant, still toiling, knowing that is who he is and not wanting to be anything else:

> Isak understood his work, his calling. He was a rich man now, with a big farm, but the heavy cash payments that had come to him by a lucky chance he used but poorly; he put the money aside. The land saved him. If he had lived down in the village, maybe the great world would have affected even him; so much gaiety, so many elegant manners and ways; he would have been buying useless trifles, and wearing a red Sunday shirt on weekdays. Here in the wilds he was sheltered from all immoderation; he lived in clear air, washed himself on Sunday mornings, and took a bath when he went up to the lake. Those thousand *Daler*—well, 'twas a gift from Heaven, to be kept intact. What else should he do? His ordinary outgoings were more than covered by the produce of his fields and stock.[41]

The copper mine, under Swedish ownership, encroached increasingly, much to the distress of the villagers. Eleseus, Isak and Inger's eldest son, having spent much time away, had returned ruined by civilization, improvident:

> Poor Eleseus, all set on end and frittered away. Better, maybe, if he'd worked on the land all the time, but now he's a man that has learned to write and use letters; no grip in him, no depth. For all that, no pitch-black devil of a man, not in love, not ambitious, hardly nothing at all is Eleseus, not even a bad thing of any great dimensions.

---

[41] Hamsun, *Growth of the Soil*, ch. 14.

> Something unfortunate, ill-fated about this young man, as if something were rotting him from within . . . the child had lost his roothold, and suffered thereby. All that he turns to now leads back to something wanting in him, something dark against the light.[42]

Eleseus represents that type which becomes predominant in the "Winter" phase of a civilization, when the city and money form the axis of living; where the peasant and the artisan emigrate from the country to the city and become either part of the rootless, alienated proletarian mass or a part of the equally rootless bourgeois. The same contrast that Hamsun dramatized was examined several years later by Spengler in his seminal study of cultural morphology, *The Decline of the West*:

> Beginning and end, a peasant cottage and a tenement-block are related to one another[43] as soul and intellect, as blood and stone. . . . Now the giant city sucks the country dry, insatiably and incessantly demanding and devouring fresh streams of men, till it wearies and dies in the midst of an almost uninhibited waste of country.[44]

Hamsun concludes with Geissler, the district official who had once come on behalf of the State to measure the worth and boundaries of Isak's land, and then to buy the copper mine from Isak, regretting the impact the mining had had

---

[42] Hamsun, *Growth of the Soil*, Book II, ch. 11.

[43] "Related to one another" in the sense that they express the analogous features of a culture in its "Spring" High Culture phase and its "Winter" Late Civilization phase respectively.

[44] Spengler, *The Decline of the West*, vol. 2, p. 102.

upon the village, offering this observation to Isak's younger son Sivert who had stayed with the land, which encapsulates Hamsun's worldview and moral of the story:

> Look at you folk at Sellanraa,[45] now; looking up at blue peaks every day of your lives; no new-fangled inventions about that, but field and rocky peaks, rooted deep in the past—but you've them for companionship. There you are, living in touch with heaven and earth, one with them, one with all these wide, deep-rooted things. No need of a sword in your hands, you go through life bareheaded, barehanded, in the midst of a great kindliness. Look, Nature's there, for you and yours to have and enjoy. Man and Nature don't bombard each other, but agree; they don't compete, race one against the other, but go together. There's you Sellanraa folk, in all this, living there. Field and forest, moors and meadow, and sky and stars—oh, 'tis not poor and sparingly counted out, but without measure. Listen to me, Sivert: you be content! You've everything to live on, everything to live for, everything to believe in; being born and bringing forth, you are the needful on earth. 'Tis not all that are so, but you are so; needful on earth. 'Tis you that maintain life. Generation to generation, breeding ever anew; and when you die, the new stock goes on. That's the meaning of eternal life. What do you get out of it? An existence innocently and properly set towards all. What do you get out of it? Nothing can put you under orders and lord it over you Sellanraa folk, you've peace and authority and this great kindliness all round. That's what you get for it. You lie at a mother's breast and suck, and play

[45] The name of Isak's farm.

> with a mother's warm hand. There's your father now, he's one of the two-and-thirty thousand. What's to be said of many another? I'm something, I'm the fog, as it were, here and there, floating around, sometimes coming like rain on dry ground. But the others? There's my son, the lightning that's nothing in itself, a flash of barrenness; he can act.
>
> My son, ay, he's the modern type, a man of our time; he believes honestly enough all the age has taught him, all the Jew and the Yankee have taught him; I shake my head at it all. But there's nothing mythical about me; 'tis only in the family, so to speak, that I'm like a fog. Sit there shaking my head. Tell the truth—I've not the power of doing things and not regretting it. If I had, I could be lightning myself. Now I'm a fog.[46]

Hamsun explicitly identified the peasantry as the wellspring of a healthy culture, the embodiment of those ever-relevant values that contrast with the values of decay represented by the city, the bourgeois, proletarianization, urbanization, and industrialization:

> A tiller of the ground, body and soul; a worker on the land without respite. A ghost risen out of the past to point the future, a man from the earliest days of cultivation, a settler in the wilds, nine hundred years old, and, withal, a man of the day.[47]

In the *August Trilogy*,[48] as in *Growth of the Soil* and else-

---

46 Hamsun, *Growth of the Soil*, Book II, ch. 12.

47 Hamsun, *Growth of the Soil*, Book II, ch. 12.

48 Knut Hamsun, *August* (1930), trans. Eugene Gay-Tifft (New York: Fertig, 1990).

where, Hamsun had taken up the concerns of encroaching mechanization and cosmopolitanism, epitomized by the US, and instead championed traditional values, such as those of localism and the rural. Nelson remarks that Hamsun was espousing an agrarian, anti-capitalist conservatism that was becoming popular among the literati in both Europe and America.

QUISLING & HITLER

With such views forming over the course of decades, and achieving wide acclaim, Hamsun's support for Quisling and for the German occupation of Norway during World War II, is consistent and principled within his historical and cultural context.

Hamsun disliked the British as much as the "Yankees" and the Bolsheviks. He had been appalled by the British war against the Boers, which he would surely have regarded as a war by a plutocratic power against an entire folk who epitomized a living remnant of the type portrayed by Isak in *Growth of the Soil*.[49] He had also alluded to the "Jews"[50] as harbingers of modernism and cosmopolitanism.

In contrast to Britain, the US, and the USSR, National Socialist Germany claimed to champion the peasantry as the eternal wellspring of a healthy culture, very much in

---

[49] The Boers were—and partly remain—an anomaly in the modern world; the vestige of the bygone era who had to be eliminated as a hindrance to the global economic structure. Hence the recent ideological and economic war against the Afrikaner to destroy apartheid was a continuation of the Boer Wars under other slogans, but with the same aim: to capture the wealth of southern Africa—in the name of "human rights"—for the sake of the same kind of plutocracy which had fought the Afrikaners' forefathers a century previously.

[50] Hamsun, *Growth of the Soil*, Book II, ch. 12.

keeping with Hamsun's views in *Growth of the Soil* and elsewhere. This is why the National Socialists saw Hamsun as a fellow-traveler.

In 1933 Walther Darré, a widely recognized agricultural expert, had been appointed Reich Minister of Food and Agriculture, and also had the title "National Peasant Leader." Goslar was named the "National Peasant City," and pageants were held to honor the peasantry. Practical measures to deal with the crisis on the land were enacted immediately, including the Hereditary Farm Law, which protected the peasantry from foreclosure and ensured the family inheritance.[51]

Alfred Rosenberg, the primary National Socialist philosopher in Germany, had already paid tribute to Hamsun in his seminal *Myth of the Twentieth Century* (1930), with specific reference to *Growth of the Soil*, as expressing the "mystical-natural will" of the peasant better than any other living artist:

> No one knows why, with great effort, the farmer Isak cultivates one piece of land after another in god-forsaken regions, or why his wife has joined him and gives birth to his children. But Isak follows an inexplicable law. He carries on a fruitful quest out of a mystical primal will. At the end of his existence he will certainly look back in astonishment at the harvest of his activity. *Growth of the Soil* is the great present day epic of the Nordic will in its eternal primordial form. Nordic man can be heroic even behind the wooden plow.[52]

---

[51] Anna Bramwell, *Blood and Soil: Richard Walther Darré and Hitler's "Green Party"* (Buckinghamshire: The Kensal Press, 1985), p. 91.

[52] Alfred Rosenberg, *The Myth of the Twentieth Century*

Such was the background when in 1934 Hamsun wrote an article, "Wait and See," in which he attacked the opponents of National Socialist Germany and asked if a return of Communists, Jews, and Heinrich Brüning to Germany were preferable. In 1935 he sent a greeting to *Der Norden*, the organ of the Nordic Society, supporting the return of the League of Nations mandate, Saarland, to Germany, and from the start supported Germany privately and publicly wherever he felt able.[53] Hamsun and his wife Marie remained particularly close to the Nordic Society, which was avid in promoting Hamsun's works.[54]

In April 1940 the Germans occupied Norway after the British had on several occasions breached Norwegian neutrality, including mining Norway's territorial waters, against which the Norwegian Government impotently protested.[55]

In 1933, former Defense Minister Vidkun Quisling had established his own party Nasjonal Samling (National Unification). Hamsun had formed a good impression of Quisling since 1932, and wrote in support of Nasjonal Samling's electoral appeal in 1936 in the party newspaper *Fritt Folk*. His wife Marie was the local representative of the party.[56]

Ironically, Quisling, whose very name became synonymous with "traitor,"[57] was the only politician who had campaigned before the war for a strong defense capability,

---

(1930), trans. Vivian Bird (Torrance, Cal.: The Noontide Press, 1982), p. 268.

53 Ferguson, *Enigma*, p. 326.

54 Ferguson, *Enigma*, p. 338.

55 Ralph Hewins, *Quisling: Prophet Without Honour* (London: W. H. Allen, 1965), p. 201. Hewins, a wartime journalist, wrote his biography to amend for the part he had played in portraying Quisling as the epitome of "treason" (p. 11).

56 Ferguson, *Enigma*, p. 333.

57 Hewins, *Quisling*, p. 9.

and was particularly pro-British, having been honored by the British Government for looking after British interests in Russia after the Bolshevik Revolution, where he had been the principal aide to the celebrated Dr. Fridtjof Nansen, who was directing the European Famine Relief to Russia in 1921, with Quisling serving as Secretary for the relief organization.[58]

Quisling sought an alliance of Nordic nations, including Germany and Britain, in what he called a "Northern Coalition" against Communism.[59]

The only strong resistance against the German invasion came from a garrison commanded by an officer who belonged to Quisling's party. The King and government quickly fled, leaving Norway without an administration or any voice to negotiate with the Germans.[60] Quisling, like Marshal Pétain in France, and many other figures throughout Europe who were to be branded and usually executed as "traitors," stepped in to fill the void as the only political figure willing to try and look after Norwegian interests under the occupation. He declared himself "minister-president," but because he was not a pliant tool he did not enjoy the confidence of the German military authorities. He was soon forced to resign in favor of an administrative council under German control, but eventually regained a measure of authority.[61]

---

58 Hewins, *Quisling*, p. 55.

59 Vidkun Quisling, *Russia and Ourselves* (London: Hodder and Stoughton, 1931), p. 275.

60 Hewins, *Quisling*, p. 208.

61 Hewins summarizes the situation when writing: "The whole myth of unprovoked aggression by Germany should be abandoned. It is incredible and does grievous injustice to the 'quislings' who are quite wrongly alleged to have engineered the German Occupation. There is no truth in this sinister legend" (*Quisling*, p. 198).

Meanwhile, Hamsun urged Norwegians to rally behind Quisling so that some form of sovereignty could be restored. He described Quisling as "more than a politician, he is a thinker, a constructive spirit."[62]

Hamsun's longest wartime article appeared in the German-language publication *Berlin-Tokyo-Rome* in February 1942, where he wrote: "Europe does not want either the Jews or their gold, neither the Americans nor their country."[63]

Despite Hamsun's pro-German sentiments, he championed the rights of his countrymen, including those who resisted the German occupation. He attempted in intercede for the writer Ronald Fangen, and many others, who had been arrested by the Gestapo.[64]

In 1943 Hamsun and his wife accepted the invitation of Goebbels to visit Germany. Goebbels wrote of Hamsun as being "the embodiment of what an epic writer should be." Hamsun was equally impressed with the Reich Minister and sent Goebbels the Nobel medal he had been awarded, which Goebbels accepted as Hamsun's "expression of solidarity with our battle for a new Europe, and a happy society."[65]

While in Germany, Hamsun met Hitler, which did not go well, as Hamsun took the opportunity to condemn the military administration of Norway which had rendered Quisling powerless. They parted in an unfriendly manner.[66]

However, Hamsun continued to support Germany, and

---

[62] Ferguson, *Enigma*, p. 357.

[63] Knut Hamsun, "Real Brotherhood," *Berlin-Tokyo-Rome*, February 1942. Quoted in Ferguson, *Enigma*, p. 365.

[64] Ferguson, *Enigma*, p. 359.

[65] Ferguson, *Enigma*, pp. 369–70.

[66] Ferguson, *Enigma*, pp. 374–75.

expressed his pride when a son, Arild, joined the Norwegian Legion of the Waffen SS.[67]

In 1945 several strokes forced Hamsun to quiet his activities. But upon Hitler's death Hamsun defiantly wrote a tribute for the press:

> I am not worthy to speak his name out loud. Nor do his life and his deeds warrant any kind of sentimental discussion. He was a warrior, a warrior for mankind, and a prophet of the gospel of justice for all nations. He was a reforming nature of the highest order, and his fate was to arise in a time of unparalleled barbarism, which finally felled him. Thus might the average western European regard Hitler. We, his closest supporters, now bow our heads at his death.[68]

Post-War Persecution

Membership in Quisling's party was declared a criminal offense and Hamsun's sons Tore and Arild[69] were among the first of 50,000 Norwegians to be arrested as "Nazis" (*sic*) or as "collaborators."[70] Marie and Knut were arrested a few weeks later. Due to his age, at 86, Hamsun was sent

---

[67] Ferguson, *Enigma*, p. 383.

[68] Knut Hamsun, "Adolf Hitler," *Aftenposten*, May 7, 1945, p. 1. Quoted in Ferguson, *Enigma*, p. 386.

[69] Ferguson, *Enigma*, p. 387.

[70] Hewins, *Quisling*, pp. 357–58. Hewins notes that these thousands of Norwegians were jailed for years often without charge or trial, interrogated for eight hours a time, subjected to "eeling" (being dragged back and forth across broken stones), and a starvation diet of 800 calories a day. "Many prisoners died of malnutrition or starvation, and limbs swollen from privation were a commonplace. Hundreds, if not thousands, died of dysentery and tuberculosis epidemics. Hundreds more bear the scars of kicking, beating, and brutality of their guards" (*Quisling*, pp. 357–58).

to a hospital rather than to a prison, although the stress and treatment struck considerably at his still quite good health. He was defiant and stated to the authorities that he would have assisted the Germans more if he could.[71]

He was sent to an old folk's home where he was a popular guest. However, prosecuting Norway's leading cultural figure, like America's dealings with Ezra Pound, was an awkward matter. Consequently, Hamsun spent 119 days in a psychiatric clinic. The psychiatrists found in him, as in the characters of his novels, a complex interplay of traits, but the most prominent of all they described was his "absolute honesty." The conclusion was that Hamsun was not insane but that he was mentally impaired. Hence, what Ferguson calls "an embarrassing situation," given that Hamsun was "first and foremost [Norway's] great writer, their national pride, a loved and admired and never quite respectable ancient child," was dealt with by concluding that his support for Germany could be put down to "senility." This was the party line taken up by the press throughout the world.[72]

Hamsun's post-war autobiographical book *On Overgrown Paths*, written amidst the threats of prosecution and the interrogations, shows him to be perfectly lucid. Although deaf and going blind, Hamsun retained his mental faculties impressively, along with a certain fatalism and humor.[73]

Although the Attorney General opted not to proceed against Hamsun, the Crown wished to try him as a member of Nasjonal Samling. To Hamsun the action at least meant that he was being officially acknowledged as of

---

[71] Ferguson, *Enigma*, pp. 387–88.

[72] Ferguson, *Enigma*, pp. 389–90.

[73] Knut Hamsun, *On Overgrown Paths* (1949) (London: MacGibbon and Kee, 1968).

sound mind. He was fined 425,000 kroner.[74]

With ruinous fines hanging over them, the Hamsuns returned to their farm Norholm.[75] On appeal the fine was reduced to 325,000 kroner,[76] his persistence and courage in speaking on behalf of imprisoned Norwegians under the German Occupation being a mitigating factor. Tore was also fined, and his brother Arild was jailed until 1949 for his membership of the Norwegian Legion. Marie Hamsun was released from jail in 1948.[77]

Although *On Overgrown Paths* was published in 1949 and became an immediate best seller,[78] Hamsun ended his days in poverty on his farm. He died in his sleep on February 19, 1952.

When Robert Ferguson's biography appeared in 1987, he wrote that although Norway is especially keen to honor its writers, "Hamsun's life remains largely uncommemorated by officialdom."[79] However, two decades later, in 2009:

> In Norway, the 150th birthday of Knut Hamsun will be celebrated by theatrical exhibitions, productions, and an international conference. One of the main squares of Oslo, located just beside the national Opera, will henceforth bear his name. A monument will finally be erected in his honor. One might say that the Norwegians have just discovered the name of their very famous compatriot. Recently, a large num-

---

[74] Ferguson, *Enigma*, p. 407.

[75] Ferguson, *Enigma*, p. 408.

[76] Ferguson, *Enigma*, p. 409.

[77] Ferguson, *Enigma*, p. 410.

[78] *On Overgrown Paths* was also published simultaneously in German and Swedish editions (Ferguson, *Enigma*, p. 416).

[79] Ferguson, *Enigma*, p. 421.

> ber of towns and villages have named squares and streets for him. At the place where he resided, in Hamaroy, a "Knut Hamsun Center" will officially open on August 4th, the day of his birth. On that day, a special postage stamp will be issued. Yet Knut Hamsun was denounced and vilified for decades by the Norwegian establishment.[80]

Hamsun's defiant commitment to Quisling and to Germany during the war was a logical conclusion to ideas that had been fermenting and widely read and applauded over a period of half a century. Yet when it came time to act on those ideals, of fighting materialism, plutocracy, and communism, for the restoration of rural and peasant values against the encroaching tide of industrialism and money, Hamsun's fellow countryman reacted with outrage. Hamsun, unlike some of the pre-war supporters of National Socialism or Fascism, for better or for worse, never did compromise his values.

---

[80] Anonymous, "Knut Hamsun: Saved by Stalin?," trans, Greg Johnson, *Counter-Currents/North American New Right,* http://www.counter-currents.com/2010/07/knut-hamsun-saved-by-stalin/. The title of the article refers to Soviet Foreign Affairs Minister Wyacheslav Molotov's intervention in favor of Hamsun in 1945, stating: "it would be regrettable to see Norway condemning this great writer to the gallows."

CHAPTER 7

EZRA POUND

"A slave is one who waits for someone else to free him."
—Ezra Pound[1]

EZRA LOOMIS POUND, 1885–1972, heralded as "a principal founder and moving spirit of modern poetry in English,"[2] was born in a frontier town in Idaho, the son of an assistant assayer and the grandson of a Congressman.

He enrolled at the University of Pennsylvania in 1901 and in 1906 was awarded his MA degree. He had already started work on his *magnum opus, The Cantos*. An avid reader of Anglo-Saxon, classical, and medieval literature, Pound continued postgraduate work on the troubadour musician-poets of medieval Provence.

Pound scholar and biographer Noel Stock was to write that Pound, when introduced to the works of Dante and of the troubadours, "wanted to devise a means of entering into the Middle Ages so as to bring them to bear upon the present,"[3] at an early stage being skeptical about the path of "progress."

In 1908 Pound traveled to Venice. There he paid $8.00 for the printing of his first volume of poetry, *A Lume Spento* (*With Tapers Quenched*).

Pound then went to London to meet W. B. Yeats and became a dominant figure in Yeats's Monday evening cir-

---

[1] Ezra Pound, *Impact: Essays on Ignorance and the Decline of American Civilization*, ed. Noel Stock (Chicago: Regnery, 1960), p. 209.

[2] *Who's Who in America*, 1969–1970.

[3] Noel Stock, *Poet in Exile: Ezra Pound* (Manchester: University of Manchester Press, 1964), p. 10.

cle, serving for a time as Yeats's secretary. He quickly gained recognition in London with the publication in 1909 of his poem *Personae* which caused a "small but definite stir."[4] He came into contact with *The English Review*, which was publishing the works of D. H. Lawrence and the author, painter, and critic Wyndham Lewis. In 1911, Pound launched his campaign for innovative writing in *The New Age* edited by the guild socialist A. R. Orage. For Pound the new poetry of the century would be "austere, direct, free from emotional slither." In considering Pound's association with T. S. Eliot, another "Rightist,"[5] Stock writes:

> The Pound-Eliot "revolution" was a return to the past in order to renew the links connecting past and present, but it also provided a new means of advance which was not available in such clear-cut form to any previous age.[6]

The following year Pound founded the Imagist movement in literature. He was by now already helping to launch the careers of William Carlos Williams, T. S. Eliot,

---

[4] Stock, *Poet in Exile*, p. 30.

[5] Eliot, like most of the individuals considered in this book, was concerned that industrialism molded "bodies of men and women—of all classes—detached from tradition, alienated from religion, and susceptible to mass suggestion: in other words a mob." Eliot advocated an organic society based on the maintenance and invigoration of classes, including the aristocratic, each with its own valuable social function. T. S. Eliot, *Notes Towards the Definition of Culture* (London: Faber & Faber, 1948), p. 48. He was not however an advocate of Fascism for Britain but believed in "Toryism," founded on religion and monarchism (Eliot, *The Criterion*, October 1931, p. 71).

[6] Stock, *Poet in Exile*, p. 55.

Ernest Hemingway, and James Joyce. He was now also the mentor of Yeats, Pound's senior by 20 years who enjoyed world recognition.

In 1914 Pound started the Vorticist movement, and although Giovanni Cianci insists that Filippo Marinetti's Futurism had a major impact on the founding of Vorticism, Futurism providing the dynamic to move beyond Imagism,[7] the English Vorticists soon broke with Marinetti, and there was frequent feuding between the two movements.[8] As Cianci concludes: "Pound was deeply immersed in the past, so that he could not welcome the Futurists' famous *antipasséism*."[9]

The original impetus for Vorticism came from the *avant-garde* sculptor Henri Gaudier-Brzeska. With Wyndham Lewis and others, he launched the magazine *Blast*. This was also the year of the world war, which took its toll on many Vorticists. The original *Blast* only went to two issues, and among the dead of the Great War was Gaudier-Brzeska. Pound was to look back, during a wartime radio address in Italy, at the Vorticist movement as an attempt at "reconstruction" in response to the "crisis OF, not IN the system . . ." But England was "too far descended into a state of flaccidity to be able to react to the medicine."[10]

---

[7] Giovanni Cianci, "Pound and Futurism," *Blast 3* (Santa Barbara: Black Sparrow Press, 1984), p. 63. *Blast 3* is a 1984 compilation of Vorticist articles by admirers of Wyndham Lewis.

[8] Eliot wrote that Pound had perhaps done more than anyone to keep Futurism out of England, and had objected to it as being "incompatible with any principle of form." Eliot, "Ezra Pound: His Metric and Poetry," 1917, reprinted in *To Criticize the Critic* (London: Faber and Faber, 1965), pp. 174–75.

[9] Cianci, "Pound and Futurism," *Blast 3*, p. 66.

[10] *Blast 3*, "Ezra Pound, Radio Speech #30," April 26, 1942, p.

Vorticism was for Pound the first major experience in revolutionary propagandizing and the first cause that placed him outside of orthodoxy. It was also Pound's last effort at "group participation in the arts, before he retreated to a position of individualism . . ."[11]

DEMOCRACY & THE RISE OF MASS MAN

Pound regarded commercialism as the force preventing the realization of his artistic-political ideal. Many others in his entourage and beyond, including Yeats and Lewis, regarded the rise of materialism, democracy, and the masses as detrimental to the arts, as newspapers and dime novels replaced literature, and the mass market determined cultural expression. Pound saw artists or what we might call the "culture-bearing strata" as a class higher than the general run of humanity who, under the regime of the democratic era, had been leveled down to a "mass of dolts," a "rabble," whose redeeming feature was to be "the waste and manure" from which grows "the tree of the arts."[12]

This revolt *against* the masses (contra the "revolt *of* the masses") at this epochal juncture became "an important linguistic project among intellectuals."[13] Virginia Woolf descried "that anonymous monster the Man in the Street" as "a vast, featureless, almost shapeless jelly of human stuff, occasionally wobbling this way or that as some instinct of hate, revenge, or admiration bubbles up beneath

---

60.

[11] Eustace Mullins, *This Difficult Individual: Ezra Pound* (Hollywood: Angriff Press, 1961), p. 88.

[12] John Carey, *The Intellectuals and the Masses: Pride and Prejudice Among the Literary Intelligentsia, 1880–1939* (London: Faber and Faber, 1992), p. 25.

[13] Carey, *The Intellectuals and the Masses*, p. 25.

it."[14] Hence, many of the cultural elite were to seek a counter-revolution in the return of aristocratic societies or saw a modern alternative in Fascism.

Pound saw it as the duty of the culture-bearing strata to rule, even dictatorially, to ensure that the arts were not swamped by mediocrity amidst the drive of business to market "culture" as another mass commodity.[15] Writing in *The Egoist* in 1914 Pound stated:

> The artist no longer has any belief or suspicion that the mass, the half-educated simpering general . . . can in any way share his delights . . . The aristocracy of the arts is ready again for its service. Modern civilization has born a race with brains like those of rabbits, and we who are the heirs of the witch doctor and the voodoo, we artists who have been so long despised are about to take over control.[16]

SOCIAL CREDIT

Pound embraced the Social Credit economic theory of Major C. H. Douglas, whom Pound met in 1917,[17] which was being promoted by A. R. Orage of *The English Review* and *The New Age*. Not only was Orage a guild socialist, but he was a primary mentor of new artists, some of whom understood the need for a new economic system in

---

[14] *The Essays of Virgina Woolf*, vol. III, 1919–1924, ed. Andrew McNeillie (London: The Hogarth Press, 1988), p. 3.

[15] That is to say, precisely the situation that has emerged, when one talks for example of the "music *industry*," or the "movie *industry*." One might just as well also state: the "art *industry*," and the "literature *industry*," as culture is now all but dominated by commercial interests.

[16] Ezra Pound, "The New Sculpture," *The Egoist*, February 16, 1914, pp. 67–68.

[17] Mullins, *This Difficult Individual*, p. 194.

order to address their concerns with the crisis in culture engendered by industrialization and plutocracy. T. S. Eliot expressed the matter cogently: "any real change for the better meant a spiritual revolution [and] that no spiritual revolution was of any use unless you had a practical economic system."[18]

Orage's backing of Douglas' monetary theory had a particularly seminal influence on Pound. Interestingly, Orage was the chief proponent of guild socialism, and his journals were considered among the foremost socialist periodicals of the day, yet even the name "Social Credit," which is generally depicted by its foes as "anti-Semitic" and crypto-Nazi,[19] was coined not by Douglas but by Orage.[20] Orage's advocacy of guild socialism, having its roots in English tradition rather than alien theorizing, would have been welcomed by certain traditionalists as providing an alternative to Marxism and capitalism, both of which are united in their materialism.

By subordinating money to the interests of society rather than allowing the power of the bankers to run unfet-

---

[18] T. S. Eliot, *The Criterion*, January 1935, p. 262.

[19] Janine Stingel, *Social Discredit: Anti-Semitism, Social Credit, and the Jewish Response* (Montreal: McGill-Queen's University Press, 2000).

[20] Some prominent advocates of "Douglas Social Credit" contend that the theory cannot be considered without reference to guild socialism and to A. R. Orage, and state that the original Social Credit articles that appeared in *The New Age* were co-written by Douglas and Orage. Orage's advocacy of Social Credit split the Fabian socialists. See Frances Hutchinson and Brian Burkitt, *The Political Economy of Social Credit and Guild Socialism* (London: Routledge, 1997). Hutchinson and Burkitt allude to the term "Social Credit" first being used by Orage. See their "Major Douglas' Proposals for a National Dividend," *International Journal of Social Economics*, 21 (1994): 19–28, n4.

tered, money would become the servant of society and not the master. Money, or more correctly, credit, would be the lubricant of commerce, a means of exchanging goods and services, rather than a profit-making commodity in itself. Hence the corrupting influence of the power of money on culture and work would be eliminated.

During the 1930s and 1940s Pound wrote a series of booklets on economics, "Money Pamphlets by £," lucidly describing economic theory and history.

Social Credit: An Impact[21] was dedicated "to the Green Shirts of England."[22] In the opening lines, Pound states that "No one can understand history without understanding economics. Gibbon's History of Rome is a meaningless jumble till a man has read Douglas."[23]

Pound pointed out the fundamentals of economic realism: that "the state has credit" and that although the sword can protect against foreign invasion, it cannot protect against the serfdom of usury, of which Pound stated: "Usury and sodomy, the Church condemned as a pair, to one hell, the same for one reason, namely that they are both against natural increase."[24]

He stated that the truth about "the principles of honest issue of money" have been known throughout history,

---

[21] Ezra Pound, *Social Credit: An Impact* (1935) (London: Peter Russell, 1951).

[22] The Green Shirts, the militant arm of Social Credit in England, marched through the streets with drums beating and banners unfurled, holding mass street rallies, publishing a newspaper, and throwing green painted bricks through bank windows to publicize their views when charges brought the perpetrators before court. It was militancy on par with Sir Oswald Mosley's Black Shirts. See K. R. Bolton, *John Hargrave and the British Greenshirts* (Paraparaumu, New Zealand: Renaissance Press, 2001).

[23] Pound, *Social Credit*, p. 1.

[24] Pound, *Social Credit*, p. 6.

but are repeatedly forgotten (or willfully obliterated), pointing to examples in history where currency has been issued without recourse to state debt. Marco Polo, for example, observed that Kublai Khan's "stamped paper money" "costs the Khan nothing" to fund his state.[25] The much-lauded "New Deal" of Pound's home country, on the other hand, indicated no comprehension of "the basic relations of currency system, money system, credit system to the needs and purchasing power of the *whole* people."[26]

Pound pointed out what should be obvious to all, namely that money—or more accurately *credit*[27]—should properly serve as a means of exchanging goods and services, and that "money is not a commodity."[28] He wrote:

> Four things are necessary in any modern or civilized economic system:
>
> 1. the labourer; 2. the product; 3. the means of transport; and 4. the monetary carrier.
>
> Inadequate monetarization has made "inaccessible islands" of fields laying adjacent one with the other; it has erected barriers between garden and factory.[29]
>
> The reason for growing food is to feed the people. The reason for weaving cloth is to clothe them. The function of a money system is to get the goods from where they are to the people who need them . . .[30]

---

[25] Pound, *Social Credit,* p. 6.

[26] Pound, *Social Credit,* pp. 6–7.

[27] There is a subtle difference between "money," or notes and coins, and "credit" or book- (today, computer)-keeping entries; most commerce is undertaken with credit rather than with notes and coins.

[28] Pound, *Social Credit,* p. 9.

[29] Pound, *Social Credit,* p. 13.

[30] Pound, *Social Credit,* p. 15.

> Money has been treated not only as if it were goods, but it has been given privileges above all other goods. This was flagrant injustice. Free men will not tolerate it for one hour after they understand it.[31]

Pound next alludes to a factor in the Great Depression that epitomizes the *criminality* of the economic system: the phenomenon of "poverty amidst plenty," which during the 1930s saw the destruction of meat and crops by government order—while people starved—because the people had no money or credit to purchase the food. One might wonder whether this was any less criminal than the planned famine in the USSR in order to destroy the *kulaks* as a class. Pound wrote of this "New Deal" economics that was supposed to secure social justice under Roosevelt: "If the American government OWNED crops sufficiently to order their destruction, it owned them quite enough to order their delivery."[32]

FASCISM

Pound considered Fascist Italy to be partially achieving Social Credit aims in breaking the power of the bankers over politics and culture, writing:

> This will not content the Douglasites nor do I believe that Douglas' credit proposals can permanently be refused or refuted, but given the possibilities of intelligence against prejudice in the year XI of the fascist era, what other government has got any further, or shows any corresponding interest in or care for the workers?[33]

---

[31] Pound, *Social Credit,* p. 15.

[32] Pound, *Social Credit,* p. 15.

[33] Ezra Pound, *Jefferson and/or Mussolini,* 1935 (New York: Liveright, 1970), p. 126.

He also saw Fascism as the culmination of an ancient tradition continued in the personalities of Mussolini, Hitler,[34] and the British Fascist leader Sir Oswald Mosley.

Pound had studied the doctrines of the ethnologist Leo Frobenius during the 1920s,[35] which gave a mystical interpretation to race and had influenced Oswald Spengler. Cultures were the product of races, and each race had its own soul, or *paideuma,* of which the artist was the guardian. In Mussolini, Pound saw not only a statesman who had overthrown the money power, but also someone who had returned culture to the center of politics. He said: "Mussolini has told his people that poetry is a necessity of state, and this displayed a higher state of civilization than in London or Washington."[36] In *Jefferson and/or Mussolini,* Pound explained:

> I don't believe any estimate of Mussolini will be valid unless it starts from his passion for construction. Treat him as *artifex* and all the details fall into place. Take him as anything save the artist and you will get muddled with contradictions . . .[37]
>
> . . . The Fascist revolution was FOR the preservation of certain liberties and FOR the maintenance of a certain level of culture, certain standards of living . . .[38]

---

[34] Pound was not originally impressed by Hitler, referring in 1935 for example to "hysterical Hitlerian yawping" (*Jefferson and/or Mussolini,* p. 127).

[35] Ezra Pound, *A Visiting Card* (Rome, 1942) (London: Peter Russell, 1952), pp. 29, 33.

[36] E. Fuller Torrey, *The Roots of Treason: Ezra Pound and the Secrets of St. Elizabeths* (London: Sidgwick and Jackson, 1984), p. 138.

[37] Pound, *Jefferson and/or Mussolini,* p. 34.

[38] Pound, *Jefferson and/or Mussolini,* p. 127.

In *Social Credit: An Impact,* published the same year, Pound wrote of Fascism in relation to economic reform:

> Fascism has saved Italy, and saving Italy bids fair to save part of Europe, but outside Italy no one has seen any fascism, only the parodies and gross counterfeits. Douglas for seventeen years has been working to build a new England and enlighten England's ex- and still annexed colonies. The corporate state[39] has invented a representative body that should function in the age of correlated machinery better than the old representation of agricultural districts.[40]

Pound saw both Italy and Japan trying to throw off the system of usury, writing: "Japan and Italy, the two really alert, active nations are both engaged in proving fragments of the Douglas analysis, and in putting bits of his scheme into practice . . ."[41]

> . . . The foregoing does not mean that Italy has gone "Social Credit." And it does not mean that I want all Englishmen to eat macaroni and sing Neapolitan love songs. It does mean or ought to mean that Englishmen are just plain stupid to lag behind Italy, the western states of America and the British Dominions . . .[42]
>
> As to your "democratic principles," the next ten

---

[39] The "corporate state" was the parliamentary structure of Fascist Italy based on occupational and professional representation rather than party representation. It was one of the syndicalist elements inherited by Fascism.

[40] Pound, *Social Credit,* p. 7.

[41] Pound, *Social Credit,* p. 19.

[42] A clear reference to the use of state credit in New Zealand, and also in Australia and Canada.

> years will show whether your groggy and incompetent parliament "represents" the will of the English people half as effectively as the new Italian Consiglio of the Guilds, where men are, at least in terms of the programme, represented by men of their own trade.[43]

It is interesting that Pound mentions Japan as having implemented some of Douglas' methods of economic policy, considering the knowledge of Japan's economic system is even more obscure to most people than those of Fascist Italy and National Socialist Germany.[44]

Douglas had toured Japan in 1929 where, as in his New Zealand tour, he was enthusiastically received. Douglas' works were published in Japan more so in any other country. In 1932 the Imperial Bank was organized as a fully state bank, and in 1942 the Bank of Japan Law was enacted, based on the 1939 Reichsbank Act in Germany.[45]

Pound and his wife Dorothy settled in Italy in 1924, "to remove himself from the deadening influence of the twentieth century's mass man."[46] He met Mussolini in 1933.[47] He also became a regular contributor to the periodicals of Mosley's British Union of Fascists,[48] first writing to Mos-

---

[43] Pound, *Social Credit*, p. 19.

[44] Bertram De Colonna, "The Truth About Germany," *The Mirror* (Auckland, New Zealand), 1938. See K. R. Bolton, *Recovery: Hitler's Financial Policy Explained* (Paraparaumu, New Zealand: Renaissance Press, 2001).

[45] Stephen M. Goodson, "Why the USA Forced the Empire of Japan into World War II," *The Barnes Review*, vol. 14, no. 6, November–December, 2008.

[46] Mullins, *This Difficult Individual: Ezra Pound*, p. 154.

[47] Torrey, *The Roots of Treason*, p. 135.

[48] *British Union Quarterly* published eight of Pound's articles between 1936–1940 (Torrey, *The Roots of Treason*, p. 137).

ley in 1934 and meeting him in 1936,[49] the latter recalling that Pound was "exactly the opposite of what I expected from the abstruse genius of his poetry. He appeared as a vivacious, bustling, and practical person . . ."[50]

Writing in Mosley's *BUF Quarterly,* Pound stated that Roosevelt and his Jewish advisers had betrayed the American Revolution.[51] It was a theme he returned to in more detail during the war: The American Revolution of 1776 had been a revolt against the control by the Bank of England of the monetary system of the American colonies. Benjamin Franklin had stated in his diary that the colonists would have gladly borne the tax on tea. They had issued their own colonial scrip. This had resulted in prosperity with a credit supply independent of the private banking system. The Bank of England intervened to compel the colonies to withdraw the scrip at a rate of devaluation that caused depression and unemployment. The colonists rebelled. But people such as Alexander Hamilton ensured that an independent America was soon again subject to the orthodox financial system of private banking control. Lincoln attempted the same resistance to the bankers and issued his famous "Lincoln Greenbacks."[52]

Pound pointed out that Mussolini had instituted banking reform in 1935 and deplored the lack of knowledge and understanding around the world of what Italy was

---

[49] Torrey, *The Roots of Treason,* p. 137.

[50] Oswald Mosley, *My Life* (London: Nelson, 1968), p. 226.

[51] Ezra Pound, "The Revolution Betrayed," *BUF Quarterly,* 1938. Reprinted in *Selections from BUF Quarterly* (Marietta, Ga.: The Truth at Last, 1995), pp. 48–55.

[52] Ezra Pound, *America, Roosevelt and the Causes of the Present War* (Venice, 1944) (London: Peter Russell, 1951). In their enthusiasm for Lincoln's "Greenbacks," monetary reformers generally do not appreciate that the Confederacy also issued its own state credit, the "Graybacks."

achieving. The US Constitution provided for the same credit system, giving the government the prerogative to create and issue its own credit and currency. Pound saw parallels between Fascist Italy and the type of economic system sought by certain American statesmen such as Jefferson and Jackson. The war was being fought in the interests of usury:

> This war was not caused by any caprice on Mussolini's part, nor on Hitler's. This war is part of the secular war between usurers and peasants, between the usurocracy and whoever does an honest day's work with his own brain or hands.[53]

In the British Union of Fascists Pound found a congenial home for his economic theories. While the policy of "state credit" advocated by fascists and National Socialists, and indeed by Pound, was not in accord with *orthodox* Social Crediters,[54] opposition to usury was a prime

---

[53] Pound, *America, Roosevelt and the Causes of the Present War,* p. 5.

[54] Orthodox Social Credit theory is *opposed* to "state credit" seeing this as akin to communism and leading to state serfdom. Any concentration of economic or political power is anathema to Social Credit orthodoxy. The orthodox viewpoint insists that "Social Credit" must be issued by an independent "credit authority" that is not associated with the state. This question however, causes considerable factionalism within Social Credit groups, which might seem analogous to the utter seriousness taken among socialist factions in their dispute over what constitutes "true Marxism." In New Zealand's successful experiment with "state credit" during the Great Depression, the primary advocate of state credit in the Labour Government, John A. Lee, commented that Douglas' *analysis* of the flaws of the financial system is valuable, and that his New Zealand tour

element of British Fascism as it was of generic fascism in most countries.

The British Union of Fascists' "director of policy," Alexander Raven Thomson, an economist who had been educated in Scotland, Germany, and the US,[55] explained that a "Fascist Government would issue the new currency and credit direct, without charge of usury . . ."[56]

Only a strong state could break the rule of the usurers, explained Thomson in a further policy pamphlet, where he pointed out that merely "nationalizing" the Bank of England would be of little use, as the bank would still be part of the international financial system, as are numerous central banks, which merely serve as the means by which the state continues to borrow from international finance. Therefore a Fascist government would bring the "control of currency out of the hands of the financial tyrants," basing credit issue on the needs of production and consumption.[57]

W. K. A. J. Chamber-Hunter[58] advocated Social Credit

---

served as the major impetus for the widespread demand for banking reform in 1934, but that the actual *methods* of implementation by the Government would have to be through a State-owned Reserve Bank. See John A. Lee, *Money Power for the People: A Policy for the Future Suggested* (Auckland: n.p., 1937), p. 4.

[55] Robert Skidelsky, *Mosley* (London: Macmillan, 1975), p. 345.

[56] Alexander Raven Thomson, *The Economics of British Fascism* (London: Bonner and Co., n.d., ca. 1935), p. 7.

[57] Alexander Raven Thomson, *Our Financial Masters* (London: British Union of Fascists, 1937), pp. 15–16.

[58] BUF Aberdeen organizer. See Stephen M. Cullen, "The Fasces and the Saltire: The Failure of the British Union of Fascists in Scotland, 1932–1940," *The Scottish Historical Journal*, 83, 2008, p. 313. Chamber-Hunter's Aberdeen branch was one of the few that were successful in Scotland, and Mosley presented

as the means by which the British Union should implement a new financial system in place of usury.[59] Thomson stated that Social Credit "deserves consideration," but that its followers failed to recognize that only strong authority could "overthrow the present financial dictatorship."[60] BUF woman's organizer Anne Brock Griggs, pointed out the suffering of mothers and children caused by the financial system due to the lack of purchasing power to buy basics such as milk, of which there was an abundance.[61] Henry Swabey traced the long tradition of the Church in condemning usury and advocating the principle of the "just price," also alluding to Douglas, and stated that the fault lies with the system that allows bankers to create credit "out of nothing as a book entry." He pointed out that in 1936 "the Bank Acts of March" in Italy enabled the state to issue credit, and not the usurer.[62]

It seems logical that Pound would have perceived the British Union as the most militant means by which to overthrow the usurers and establish a just social system, together with the examples of Germany and Italy as having introduced measures in that direction. Hence he wrote in 1939: "USURY is the cancer of the world, which only the surgeon's knife of Fascism can cut out of the life of nations."[63]

---

him with the BUF Gold Award in 1937. He resigned from the BUF in 1939 "to pursue his interest in Social Credit (*ibid.*, p. 316).

[59] W. K. A. J. Chamber-Hunter, *British Union and Social Credit* (London: British Union, ca. 1938).

[60] Alexander Raven Thomson, "Causes of the Slump," *BUF Quarterly*, 1937; *Selections from BUF Quarterly*, p. 20.

[61] Anne Brock Griggs, "Food or Usury?," *BUF Quarterly*, 1936; *Selections from BUF Quarterly*, pp. 34–37.

[62] Henry Swabey, "From Just Price to Usury," *BUF Quarterly*, 1939; *Selections from BUF Quarterly*, pp. 71–78.

[63] Ezra Pound, *What is Money For?* (1939) (London: Peter

Pound's Canto XLV, "With Usura," is a particularly lucid exposition of how the usury system infects social and cultural bodies. He provides a note at the end defining usury as "a charge for the use of purchasing power, levied without regard to production: often without regard even to the possibilities of production."

With usura . . .
no picture is made to endure nor to live with
but it is made to sell and to sell quickly
with usura, sin against nature,
is thy bread ever more of stale rags
is thy bread dry as paper, . . .
and no man can find site for his dwelling.
Stone cutter is kept from his stone
weaver is kept from his loom
WITH USURA
wool comes not to market
sheep bringeth no gain with usura . . .
Usura rusteth the chisel
It rusteth the craft and the craftsman
It gnaweth the thread in the loom . . .
Usura slayeth the child in the womb
It stayeth the young man's courting
It hath brought palsey to bed, lyeth
between the young bride and her bridegroom
CONTRA NATURAM
They have brought whores to Eleusis
Corpses are set to banquet
at behest of usura.[64]

Russell, 1951), p. 12.

[64] *Ezra Pound: Selected Poems, 1908–1959* (London: Faber & Faber, 1975), "Canto XLV: With Usura," pp. 147–48.

"With Usura" precisely reflects Pound's position that the financial system denies the cultural heritage and creativity of the people, creates poverty amidst plenty, and fails to act as a mechanism for the exchange of the productive and cultural heritage, by making credit a commodity instead of a means of exchange. Creativity either fails to reach its destination or is stillborn. We might with this poem in particular understand why Pound felt the problem of banking and credit to be of crucial concern to artists.

Caged

From the late 1930s Pound began to look with favor at the economic system created by Hitler's regime and regarded the Rome-Berlin Axis as "the first serious attack on usurocracy since the time of Lincoln." Several years after referring to "hysterical Hitlerian yawping,"[65] and by this time aware of the war that was being agitated against Germany, Pound quoted from *Mein Kampf* in regard to usury:

> The struggle against international finance and loan capital has become the most important point in the National Socialist programme: the struggle of the German nation for its independence and freedom.[66]

In April 1939 Pound went to the US to try and garner support against America's entry into a war that he saw was approaching against Germany. He told Archibald MacLeish[67] during an interview for the *Atlantic Monthly*, that he had not come to the US to talk about literature, but

---

[65] Pound, *Jefferson and/or Mussolini*, p. 127.

[66] Ezra Pound, *What is Money For?*, p. 12.

[67] MacLeish also supported Social Credit.

to convince his countrymen to keep out of any European conflagration, in the hope that if war could not be averted, it could at least be confined.[68]

In 1940, after having returned to Italy, Pound offered his services as a radio broadcaster. The broadcasts, called "The American Hour," began in January 1941.[69]

In July 1943 Mussolini was deposed, and Pound was indicted for treason by a grand jury in the District of Columbia, along with seven Americans who had been broadcasting for Germany. Hemingway, concerned at the fate of his old mentor after the war, suggested the possibility of an "insanity" plea,[70] and the idea caught on among some of his literary friends who had obtained good jobs in the US government.[71] Other interests were pressing for the death penalty.

With the American invasion, Pound headed for the Salò Republic, the Fascist last stand, where he wrote a flow of articles, mostly on economic reform, and in December, 1943 resumed his radio broadcasts.

Mussolini was murdered on April 28, 1945. On May 2, Pound was taken from his home by Italian partisans after he had unsuccessfully attempted to turn himself over to the American forces. Putting a book of Confucius into his pocket, he went with the partisans expecting to be hanged, as a bloodlust was now turned against those who had been loyal to Mussolini.[72] Instead, he ended up in an American camp at Pisa constructed for the most vicious military prisoners. Pound was confined in a bare iron

---

[68] Mullins, *This Difficult Individual*, pp. 196–97.

[69] Torrey, *The Roots of Treason*, p. 158.

[70] Torrey, *The Roots of Treason*, p. 175.

[71] MacLeish had become assistant secretary in the US State Department.

[72] Torrey, *The Roots of Treason*, p. 176.

cage in the burning heat, sleeping on the concrete floor, brilliantly lighted throughout the night. This was what Pound later called the "gorilla cage." *Esquire* commented: "The dust and the light soon became intolerable; he became physically very weak; he lost his memory, eventually he broke down."[73]

He was transferred to a medical facility and lived in a small tent. "Despite his extraordinary predicament, Pound's native spirit soon returned and he was writing his new Cantos."[74]

In November 1945, he was flown to Washington and jailed. While Hemingway, *et al.* had planned to have Pound declared "insane" to avoid treason charges, the conditions he had been subjected to had in fact caused him to mentally and physically break down, and by the time he reached Washington his lawyer, Julien Cornell, described Pound as being "in a rather desperate condition."[75] On December 21 he was sent to St. Elizabeths mental hospital. Again, conditions were atrocious. The ward was for the criminally insane, and "reeked of sweat and urine." He lived in fear of the other inmates. On February 13, 1946, formal hearings declared him to be of unsound mind, and was kept at St. Elizabeths for eleven years.[76] Here his literary output continued, and he translated 300 traditional Chinese poems that were published by Harvard University Press in 1954.[77] He was awarded the Bollingen Prize for Poetry in 1949 for the "Pisan Cantos," the award causing uproar amidst accusations of

---

[73] Peter Ackroyd, *Ezra Pound and His World* (London: Thames and Hudson, 1989), p. 86.

[74] Ackroyd, *Ezra Pound and His World,* p. 86.

[75] Ackroyd, *Ezra Pound and His World,* p. 91.

[76] Ackroyd, *Ezra Pound and His World,* p. 92.

[77] Torrey, *The Roots of Treason*, p. 222.

"Fascist infiltrators," but scholarly interest in Pound increased widely.[78] Others tried to consign him to oblivion.[79]

In 1958, the indictment for treason was dropped, after years of campaigning for his release by influential friends such as Eliot, MacLeish, Robert Frost, Congressman Usher L. Burdick,[80] and even UN Secretary General Dag Hammarskjöld who maintained a correspondence with Pound and was among those campaigning for Pound's nomination for the Nobel Prize in Literature.[81]

Throughout his ordeal, Pound maintained his political beliefs, and among the visitors to St. Elizabeths seeking the wisdom of "Granpaw" was John Kasper, a fiery young intellectual and admirer of Pound's poetry who became well-known for his tours of the South defending segregation. Kasper saw Pound frequently and maintained a weekly correspondence. Kasper became Pound's protégé. He established a right-wing bookshop and a publishing venture under Pound's guidance, the "Square Dollar Series." Kasper's strident pro-segregation leaflets, which he distributed throughout the South, were inspired by Pound's poetic style.[82]

When Pound was released after thirteen years of confinement, eleven in an asylum, journalists who interviewed him concluded that Pound, while eccentric, did not display any signs of insanity.[83]

---

[78] Ackroyd, *Ezra Pound and His World*, p. 96.

[79] Random House refused to include any works by Pound in a poetry anthology, although one of the editors had chosen twelve of Pound's poems for inclusion. Charles Norman, *Ezra Pound* (New York: Macmillan, 1960), p. 416.

[80] Ackroyd, *Ezra Pound and His World*, p. 98.

[81] Torrey, *The Roots of Treason*, pp. 254–55.

[82] Torrey, *The Roots of Treason*, pp. 228–29.

[83] Torrey, *The Roots of Treason*, p. 262.

On June 30, 1958, Pound set sail for Italy. When he reached Naples, he gave the Fascist salute to journalists and declared, "all America is an insane asylum."[84] He continued with *The Cantos* and stayed in contact with political personalities such as Kasper and Mosley. He remained defiantly opposed to the American system when giving interviews, despite the protests of US diplomats to the Italian government.

In 1951, Peter Russell, a London publisher, reprinted many of Pound's pamphlets on economics, which he stated was "essential to the full understanding of [Pound's] major poetical work, *The Cantos*." Russell commented that although the publication of the pamphlets had no political motive, they are "a healthy reaction . . . to the vicious plutocracy and the destructive bureaucracy which seem today to be the twin tyrants of our uneasy world."[85]

Pound continued to write for Mosley as he had before the war, which drew the interest of a new generation of admirers of Pound's poetry,[86] including the scholars Alan Neame, Noel Stock,[87] and Denis Goacher.[88] A 1959 issue of Mosley's journal, *The European*,[89] carries Pound's "Ci de

---

[84] Torrey, *The Roots of Treason*, p. 263.

[85] Peter Russell, "Publisher's Note," 1950, Ezra Pound, *Social Credit: An Impact*.

[86] Skidelsky, *Mosley*, pp. 493–94.

[87] Stock authored *The Life of Ezra Pound* (New York: Random House, 1970) and *Poet in Exile: Ezra Pound*.

[88] Goacher, the British actor and poet, went to Washington in 1953 and became Pound's secretary, typing his poetry and essays. He was important in campaigning for Pound's release and thereafter visited Pound in Italy. Goacher became "drama critic" for Mosley's *European*. See Nicholas Johnson, "Obituary: Denis Goacher," *The Independent*, May 6, 1998.

[89] Ezra Pound, "Ci de los Cantares," *The European*, vol. 12, no. 6, February 1959, pp. 382–84. This issue also carries a re-

los Cantares," a mixture of Chinese characters and terms as well as references to Yeats, bygone statesmen, percentages and prices, and non-usurious banking practices: "Gaudin did not pay interest on government credit. Nor did Kang Hi."

Pound died on November 1, 1972, "the last of a generation which had tried to create art and literature on an heroic scale."[90]

---

view by Alan Neame of Ronald Firbank's play, "Valmouth" (p. 372). Also in this issue is a revisionist article by Noel Stock, citing Harry Elmer Barnes, discussing financial sources for the Russian Revolution, and alluding Poundian-style to usury as the cause of civilizational collapse ("Blackout on History," pp. 337–43). Alan Neame's poem "Levant Elevenses," appears in the July 1958 issue of *The European*, vol. 11, no. 5, p. 305. Denis Goacher's poem, "In Memoriam *New Statesman*," satirizes the bourgeois liberal of that magazine, and spoofs their obliviousness to the cultural decay of Britain, with its "rock and roll" and "stereophonic crooning . . ." (vol. 12, no. 4, December 1958, pp. 250–51).

[90] Ackroyd, *Ezra Pound and His World*, p. 115.

CHAPTER 8

WYNDHAM LEWIS

WYNDHAM LEWIS, 1882–1957, is credited with founding the only modernist cultural movement indigenous to Britain. Nonetheless, he is seldom spoken of in the same breath as Ezra Pound, James Joyce, T. S. Eliot, and others of his generation.[1] Lewis was one of a number of cultural figures who rejected the legacy of nineteenth-century bourgeois liberalism and democracy that had descended on the twentieth.

However, unlike many other writers who eschewed democracy, liberalism, and "the Left," Lewis also rejected the counter-movement that sought to return to the past and embrace the intuitive, the emotional, and the instinctual above the intellectual and the rational. Lewis particularly denounced D. H. Lawrence for his espousal of instinct above reason and for what appeared to be a celebration of the doctrine of the "noble savage," which has served as the basis of liberalism from the eighteenth century on.

Lewis was an extreme individualist, while rejecting the individualism of nineteenth-century liberalism. His espousal of a philosophy of distance between the cultural elite and the masses brought him to Nietzsche, although he was appalled by the popularity of Nietzsche among all and sundry,[2] and to Fascism and the praise of Hitler, but to the

---

[1] Frederic Jameson, *Fables of Aggression: Wyndham Lewis, the Fascist as Modernist* (Berkeley: University of California Press, 1981), p. 1.

[2] In the Preface to *Tarr: The 1918 Version,* ed. Paul O'Keefe (Santa Barbara, Cal.: Black Sparrow Press, 1990) Lewis laments that Nietzscheanism has "made an Over-man of every vulgarly energetic grocer in Europe."

rejection of these also as appealing to the masses.

Born in 1882 on a yacht off the shores of Nova Scotia, his mother was English, his father an eccentric American army officer without income who soon deserted the family. Wyndham and his mother arrived in England in 1888. He attended Rugby and the Slade School of Art,[3] both of which obliged him to leave. He then wandered the art capitals of Europe being influenced by Cubism and Futurism.

In 1922, Lewis exhibited his portfolio of drawings that had been intended to illustrate an edition of Shakespeare's *Timon of Athens*, in which Timon is depicted as a snapping puppet. This illustrated Lewis's view that man can rise above the animal by classical detachment and control, but that the majority of men will always remain as puppets or automata. Having read Nietzsche, Lewis was intent on remaining a Zarathustrian figure, solitary upon his mountaintop far above the mass of humanity.

VORTEX

Lewis was originally associated with the Bloomsbury group, the pretentious and snobbish intellectual denizens of a delineated area of London who could make or break an aspiring artist or writer. He soon rejected these parlor pink liberals and vehemently attacked them in *The Apes of God*.[4] This resulted in a turning point—a downward turn—in Lewis's career: "Raucous controversy followed." The manuscript had been rejected by Lewis's publisher, Chatto and Windus, and he had published the book himself under the imprint of "The Arthur Press." Matters were not helped by Lewis's *Hitler* in 1931. His close supporter Roy Campbell

---

3 William H. Pritchard, *Wyndham Lewis* (London: Routledge and Kegan Paul, 1972), p. 2.

4 Wyndham Lewis, *The Apes of God* (1932) (Santa Barbara, Cal.: Black Sparrow Press, 1984).

was also dragged down with him,[5] although Campbell would clearly have suffered the same opposition from Bloomsbury because of his own views.

One biographer has written: "The triumphs of the late twenties, triumphs which included generally favorable critical response . . . were temporarily forgotten in the critical-legal-popular-cat hullabaloo . . . ," and Lewis became a "bad risk" for publishers.[6] Bloomsbury was a powerful coterie that "could go so far as to excommunicate and to ostracize."[7]

> To stand out against this kind of opposition was not easy. Yet that was precisely what Lewis did, despite lack of funds and a refusal to throw himself on the mercy of "well-connected" persons. During the 1930s, when it was the fashion in Britain to assume a left-wing viewpoint, Lewis would have none of it.[8]

E. W. F. Tomlin remarks on Lewis's revolt against the fashionable Left and its relevance today:

> When one reflects upon the radical political sympathies displayed by men who have since joined the Establishment, Lewis's own refusal to be badgered, jockeyed, or inveigled into alliance with the left-wing intelligentsia shows stoutness of character and independence of spirit. And now that a New Left has aris-

---

[5] Bradford Morrow, "A History of an Unapologetic Apologia: Roy Campbell's Wyndham Lewis," *Blast 3* (Santa Barbara, Cal.: Black Sparrow Press, 1984), p. 11.

[6] Morrow, "A History of an Unapologetic Apologia," p. 11.

[7] E. W. F. Tomlin, "Wyndham Lewis: The Emancipator," *Blast 3*, p. 109.

[8] Tomlin, "Wyndham Lewis: The Emancipator," p. 110.

> en, Lewis's work possesses fresh relevance especially as today's radicalism combines its assault upon the "foundations of society" with the most pitiful essays in the scabrous. . . . How Lewis would have trounced it all . . .[9]

Breaking with Bloomsbury's Omega Workshop, Lewis founded the Rebel Art Centre from which emerged the Vorticist movement and their magazine *Blast: Review of the Great English Vortex,*[10] "blowing away dead ideas and worn-out notions," as Lewis put it.[11] Signatories to the Vorticist Manifesto included Ezra Pound, French sculptor Henri Gaudier-Brzeska, and painter Edward Wadsworth. T. S. Eliot was also an adherent, contributing articles to *Blast* 2.[12]

Pound, who described the vortex as "the point of maximum energy," coined the name Vorticism. Although Lewis had found both the stasis of Cubism and the frenzied movement of Futurism interesting, he became indignant at Marinetti's description of him as a Futurist and wished to found an indigenous English modernist movement. The aim was to synthesize Cubism and Futurism.[13] Vorticism would depict the static point from which energy arose. It was also very much concerned to reflect contemporary life where the machine was coming to dominate but rejected Futurism's romantic glorification of the machine.[14]

Both Pound and Lewis were influenced by the Classicism of the art critic and philosopher T. E. Hulme, a radical

---

[9] Tomlin, "Wyndham Lewis: The Emancipator," p. 110.

[10] William C. Wees, "Wyndham Lewis and Vorticism," *Blast 3,* p. 47.

[11] Wees, "Wyndham Lewis and Vorticism," p. 49.

[12] *Blast* 2 (Santa Barbara, Cal.: Black Sparrow Press, 1981).

[13] Wees, "Wyndham Lewis and Vorticism," p. 48.

[14] Wees, "Wyndham Lewis and Vorticism," p. 49.

conservative. Hulme rejected nineteenth-century humanism and romanticism in the arts as reflections of the Rousseauian (and ultimately communistic) belief in the natural goodness of man when uncorrupted by civilization, and of human nature as infinitely malleable by a change of environment and social conditioning. Hulme writes:

> . . . People of all classes, people who stood to lose by it, were in a positive ferment about the idea of liberty. There must have been some idea which enabled them to think that something positive could come out of so essentially negative a thing. There was, and here I get my definition of romanticism. They had been taught by Rousseau that man was by nature good, that it was only bad laws and customs that had suppressed him. Remove all these and the infinite possibilities of man would have a chance. This is what made them think that something positive could come out of disorder, this is what created the religious enthusiasm. Here is the root of all romanticism: that man, the individual, is an infinite reservoir of possibilities; and if you can so rearrange society by the destruction of oppressive order then these possibilities will have a chance and you will get Progress.
>
> One can define the classical quite clearly as the exact opposite to this. Man is an extraordinarily fixed and limited animal whose nature is absolutely constant. It is only by tradition and organisation that anything decent can be got out of him.
>
> . . . Put shortly, these are the two views, then. One, that man is intrinsically good, spoilt by circumstance; and the other that he is intrinsically limited, but disciplined by order and tradition to something fairly decent. To the one party man's nature is like a well, to the other like a bucket. The view which regards man

> as a well, a reservoir full of possibilities, I call the romantic; the one which regards him as a very finite and fixed creature, I call the classical.[15]

Hulme makes it clear that "romanticism" is the dogmatic underpinning of the dominant liberal paradigm of Western societies.

Lewis's classicism is constructed around a set of dichotomies: classicism versus romanticism, reason versus emotion, intellect versus intuition and instinct, masculine versus feminine, aristocracy versus democracy, the individual versus the masses, and later fascism versus communism. The Vorticist aesthetic lent itself readily to proto-fascist and conservative interpretations: "disciplined, blunt, thick, and brutal" designs, clarity and form as opposed to the art that dissolves in the "vagueness of space," as Lewis described it.[16]

Artistically, classicism also meant clarity of style and distinct form. Pound was drawn to the manner in which, for example, Chinese ideograms depicted ideas succinctly.[17] Hence, art and writing were to be based on terseness and clarity of image. The subject was viewed externally in a detached manner. Pound and Hulme had founded the Imagist movement on classicist lines. This was now superseded by Vorticism, depicting the complex but clear geometrical patterns of the machine age. In contradiction to Italian Futurism, Vorticist art aimed not to depict the release of

---

[15] T. E. Hulme, "Romanticism and Classicism," *Speculations* (1911), (New York: Harcourt, Brace and World, 1936), p. 114.

[16] Wees, "Wyndham Lewis and Vorticism," p. 49.

[17] See for example the Chinese ideograms illustrating the concept of Confucian social order in Pound's *Jefferson and/or Mussolini* (New York: Liveright, 1970), ch. 29, "Kung," which he equates with Fascist order. Also the Chinese ideograms used in Pound's Cantos LI and LIII.

energy but to freeze it in time. While depicting the swirl of energy, the central axis of stability distinguished Vorticism from Futurism. Vorticism was however rejected by Lewis during the course of the First World War as being "bleak and empty," as something that needed "filling," while in literature, words and syntax should not be subjects of abstraction.[18]

In his novel *Tarr*, published as a monument to himself should he be killed in the war in which he served as a forward observation officer with the artillery, he lambastes the bohemian artists and literati exemplified in England by the Bloomsbury coterie:

> . . . Your flabby potion is a mixture of the lees of Liberalism, the poor froth blown off the decadent Nineties, the wardrobe-leavings of a vulgar bohemianism. . . . You are concentrated, highly-organized barley water: there is nothing in the universe to be said for you: any efficient state would confiscate your property, burn your wardrobe—that old hat and the rest—as infectious, and prohibit you from propagating.
>
> . . . A breed of mild pervasive cabbages has set up a wide and creeping rot in the West . . . that any resolute power will be able to wipe up overnight, with its eyes shut. Your kind meantime make it indirectly a peril and tribulation for live things to remain in your neighborhood. You are systematizing and vulgarizing the individual: you are the advance-copy of communism, a false millennial middle-class communism. You are not an individual: you have, I repeat, no right to that hair and to that hat: you are trying to have the

---

[18] Wyndham Lewis, *Rude Assignment: A Narrative of My Career Up-to-Date* (London: Hutchinson, 1950), p. 129.

> apple and eat it too. You should be in uniform and at work, *not* uniformly *out of uniform* and libelling the Artist by your idleness. Are you idle?
>
> ... The only justification of your slovenly appearance it is true is that it is perfectly emblematic.[19]

In 1918, Lewis was commissioned as an official war artist for the Canadian War Records Office. Here some of his paintings are in the Vorticist style, depicting soldiers as machines of the same quality as their artillery. Again, man is shown as an automaton. However, the war destroyed the Vorticist movement, Hulme and Gaudier-Brzeska both succumbing, and *Blast* did not go beyond two issues.

THE CODE OF A HERDSMAN

Lewis's neo-Nietzscheanism is succinctly expressed in an essay published in *The Little Review* in 1917, "The Code of a Herdsman." Among the 18 points:

> In accusing yourself, stick to the Code of the Mountain. But crime is alien to a Herdsman's nature. Your self must be your Caste.
>
> Cherish and develop side by side, your six most constant indications of different personalities. You will then acquire the potentiality of six men ... Each trench must have another one behind it.
>
> Spend some of your time every day in hunting your weaknesses caught from commerce with the herd, as methodically, solemnly and vindictively as a monkey his fleas. You will find yourself swarming with them while you are surrounded by humanity. But you must not bring them up on the mountain ...

---

[19] Wyndham Lewis, *Tarr* (1918) (Harmondsworth: Penguin Books, 1982), pp. 25–26.

> Do not play with political notions, aristocratisms, or the reverse, for that is a compromise with the herd. Do not allow yourself to imagine a fine herd though still a herd. There is no fine herd. The cattle that call themselves "gentlemen" you will observe to be a little cleaner. It is merely cunning and produced by a product called soap . . .
>
> Be on your guard with the small herd of gentlemen. There are very stringent regulations about the herd keeping off the sides of the mountain. In fact your chief function is to prevent their encroaching. Some in moments of boredom or vindictiveness are apt to make rushes for the higher regions. Their instinct fortunately keeps them in crowds or bands, and their trespassing is soon noted. Contradict yourself. In order to live you must remain broken up.
>
> Above this sad commerce with the herd, let something veritably remain "*un peu sur la montagne.*" Always come down with masks and thick clothing to the valley where we work. Stagnant gasses from these Yahooesque and rotten herds are more dangerous than the wandering cylinders that emit them. . . . Our sacred hill is a volcanic heaven. But the result of the violence is peace. The unfortunate surge below, even, has moments of peace. [20]

"The Code of a Herdsman" seems particularly reminiscent of Nietzsche's "Of the Flies of the Market Place" in *Thus Spoke Zarathustra*.[21] The credo also indicates why Lewis could not stay an admirer of Fascism or National

---

[20] Wyndham Lewis, "The Code of a Herdsman" can be read at: http://www.gingkopress.com/09-lit/code-of-herdsman.html

[21] Friedrich Nietzsche, *Thus Spoke Zarathustra*, trans. R. J. Hollingdale (Harmondsworth: Penguin, 1969), pp. 78–81.

Socialism for long —"Do not allow yourself to imagine a fine herd though still a herd. There is no fine herd."— since Fascism and National Socialism elevate the "herd," culturally, socially, and economically.

FASCISM

Poverty dogged Lewis all his life. He, like Pound, looked for a society that would honor artists. Like Pound and D. H. Lawrence, he felt that the artist is the natural ruler of humanity, and he resented the degradation of art to a commodity.

Lewis's political and social outlook arises from his aesthetics. He was opposed to the primacy of politics and economics over cultural life. His 1926 book *The Art of Being Ruled* details Lewis's ideas on politics, including a rejection of democracy and some favorable references to Fascism. Here Lewis condemns the vulgarization of Science as a "popular religion," conducive to a "revolutionary state of mind," and the myth of "Progress,"[22] based on the idolization of "mechanical betterment."[23] The ideal is the "Man in the Street" as "the new Messiah of contemporary religion," who is continuously being sold the idea of change, or "revolution-as-habit."[24] Lewis as a revolutionary was concerned with overthrowing "outworn values," and was antithetical to the "revolution-as-habit" of the stereotypical intellectuals of the Bloomsbury type.[25]

He also offers a skeptical analysis regarding the purposes of "democracy" where power is exercised behind the illusion of free elections, which are based on the conditioning of the voting mass by the owners of the Press, that is to

---

22 Roy Campbell, "Wyndham Lewis," *Blast 3*, p. 15.

23 Campbell, "Wyndham Lewis," p. 23.

24 Campbell, "Wyndham Lewis," p. 16.

25 Campbell, "Wyndham Lewis," p. 18.

say, those who have the money:

> The working of the "democratic" electoral system is of course as follows: A person is trained up stringently to certain opinions; then he is given a vote, called a "free" and fully enfranchised person; then he votes (subject, of course, to new and stringent orders from the press, where occasionally his mentor commands him to vote contrary to what he has been taught) strictly in accordance with his training. His support for everything that he has been taught to support can be practically guaranteed. Hence, of course, the vote of the free citizen is a farce: education and suggestion, the imposition of the will of the ruler through the press and other publicity channels, canceling it. So "democratic" government is far more effective than subjugation by physical conquest.[26]

Support for Fascism was a product of his Classicism—his valorization of the hard, the masculine, the clear, and the exact—as well as his long-held opinions regarding democracy and the masses. This classicism prompted him to applaud the "rigidly organized" fascist state, based on changeless, absolute laws that Lewis applied to the arts, in opposition to the "flux" or changes of romanticism.

Lewis supported Sir Oswald Mosley's British Union of Fascists. Mosley relates in his autobiography how Lewis would secretly arrange to meet him, fearing assassination.[27] However, Lewis was open enough to write an essay on Fascism entitled "Left Wings," for *British Union Quarterly*. Here Lewis writes that a nation can be subverted and taken

---

[26] Wyndham Lewis, *The Art of Being Ruled* (London: Chatto & Windus, 1926), p. 111.

[27] Oswald Mosley, *My Life* (London: Nelson, 1968), p. 225.

over by numerically small groups. The intelligentsia and the press were doing this work of subversion with a left wing orientation. Lewis was aware of the backing Marxism was receiving from the wealthy, including the millionaire bohemians who patronized the arts. Marxist propaganda in favor of the USSR amounted to vast sums financially. Marxism is a sham, a masquerade in its championship of the poor against the rich.[28] "Russian communism is not a war-to-the-knife of the Rich against the Poor is only too plainly demonstrated by the fact that internationally all the Rich are on its side. All the 'magnates' among the nations are for it; all the impoverished communities, all the small peasant States, dread and oppose it."[29]

Lewis's observations on the nature of Marxism were borne out by the anti-Bolshevist stance of Portugal and Spain, which is presumably what he means by the opposition of "small peasant states" to communism. While Bolshevism itself was funded by financial circles in New York, Sweden, and Germany (the Warburgs, Jacob Schiff, and Olaf Aschberg, the so-called "Bolshevik Banker"[30]), hence the claim "the 'magnates' amongst the nations are for it."

Lewis concludes by declaring Fascism to be the movement that is genuinely for the poor against the rich, for property while the "super-rich" are against property, "since money has merged into power, the concrete into the abstract . . ."

---

[28] Wyndham Lewis, "Left Wings," *British Union Quarterly*, January–April 1937, in *Selections from BUF Quarterly* (Marietta, Ga.: The Truth at Last, 1995), p. 137.

[29] Lewis, "Left Wings," *British Union Quarterly*, p. 137.

[30] K. R. Bolton, "November 1917: Wall Street and the November 1917 Bolshevik Revolution," *Ab Aeterno*, no. 5, October-December 2010.

> You as a Fascist stand for the small trader against the chain store; for the peasant against the usurer: for the nation, great or small, against the super-state; for personal business against Big Business; for the craftsman against the Machine; for the creator against the middleman; for all that prospers by individual effort and creative toil, against all that prospers in the abstract air of High Finance or of the theoretic ballyhoo of Internationalism.[31]

As indicated by his references to "High Finance" and the "magnates" supporting the Left, Lewis, like Ezra Pound,[32] was aware of the base rot of the financial system founded on usury, writing: "the technique of Credit is an instrument of destruction in comparison with which every other known weapon of offence shrinks into insignificance."[33]

Nonetheless, Lewis had reservations about Fascism just as he had reservations about commitment to any doctrine, not only because of the mass—or "herd"—nature of Fascism, but because the principle of action, of the man of action, becomes too much of a frenzied activity, where stability in the world is needed for the arts to flourish. He states in *Time and Western Man* that Fascism in Italy stood too much for the past, with emphasis on a resurgence of the Roman imperial splendor and the use of its imagery, rather than the realization of the present.[34] As part of the "Time

---

31 Lewis, "Left Wings," p. 137.

32 Yet he rejected Pound's admonition to study C. H. Douglas' Social Credit economics and referred to "credit-cranks"—Lewis, *The Hitler Cult* (London: Dent, 1939), p. 26, apparently not offering a practical alternative to what he also termed "Credit Kings" and the "Emperors of Debt." See Wyndham Lewis, *Doom of Youth* (New York: McBride, 1932), p. 35.

33 Lewis, *Doom of Youth*, p. 35.

34 Paradoxically, Lewis, despite his support for Hitler and

cult," it was in the doctrinal stream of action, progress, violence, struggle, of constant flux in the world, that also includes Darwinism and Nietzscheanism despite the continuing influence of the latter on Lewis's own philosophy.

Yet when the lines were being drawn for the coming confrontation between Fascism and democracy, Lewis went to the defense of Fascist Italy's invasion of Abyssinia, condemning the League of Nations sanctions against Italy and stating, "that the industrious and ingenious Italian, rather than the lazy, stupid, and predatory Ethiopian, should eventually control Abyssinia is surely not such a tragedy."[35]

An early appreciation entitled *Hitler* was published in 1931, sealing Lewis's fate as a neglected genius, despite his repudiation of anti-Semitism in *The Jews, Are They Human?* and National Socialism in *The Hitler Cult*, both published in 1939.

TIME & SPACE

A healthy artistic environment requires order and discipline, not chaos and flux. This is the great conflict between the "romantic" and the "classical" in the arts. This "classical" and "romantic" dichotomy is represented in politics as the difference between the philosophy of "Time" and of "Space," the former of which is epitomized in the philosophy of Spengler. Unlike many others of the "Right," Lewis was vehemently opposed to the historical approach of Spengler, critiquing his *Decline of the West* in *Time and Western Man*. To Lewis, Spengler and other "Time philoso-

---

Mosley, had never supported Italian Fascism, regarding it as being "political futurism." Bryant Knox, "Ezra Pound on Wyndham Lewis's Rude Assignment," *Blast 3*, p. 161.

[35] Wyndham Lewis, *Left Wings Over Europe* (London: Jonathan Cape, 1936), pp. 164–65.

phers" relegated culture to the political sphere. The cyclic and organic interpretations of history are seen as "fatalistic" and demoralizing to the survival of the European race. Lewis summed up Spengler's thesis as, "you White Peoples are about to be extinguished. It's all up with you; and I can prove to you on the testimony of my data of research, and according to my new science of history, which is built on the great time-system . . ."[36]

Lewis claimed that "Time philosophy" is committed to ongoing change and flux, whereas the philosophy of "Space" is committed to form and presence, the foundations of classicism, which Spengler disparaged in favor of the formless infinite yearning of "Faustian" man.[37]

True art is not revolutionary, but is a "constant stronghold," that is never in revolt except when art ceases to exist or becomes "spurious and vulgar." The so-called "revolutionary art" that Lewis observed in his time was "either inferior and stupid, or else consciously political, art."[38] Lewis writes, furthermore, that: "No artist can ever love democracy or its doctrinaire and more primitive relative, communism."

> The emotionally-excited, closely-packed, heavily-standardized mass-units, acting in a blind, ecstatic unison, as though in response to the throbbing of some unseen music—of the sovietic . . . fancy—would be the last thing, according to me, for the free democratic West to aim for, *if* it were free, and *if* its democ-

---

[36] Wyndham Lewis, *Time and Western Man* (London: Chatto & Windus, 1927), p. 262.

[37] Spengler did not "disparage" other cultures; he sought to describe their inner essence as a detached observer.

[38] Lewis, *Time and Western Man,* pp. 39–40.

racy were of an intelligent order . . .[39]

Lewis regarded the "revolutionary" movements as regressive, despite their being termed "progressive." Feminism aims to return to the "supposed conditions of the primitive Matriarchate." Communism and all revolutionary movements of his time, he regarded as aiming to return to the primitive.[40] On this rationale, one can see why he also condemned D. H. Lawrence. "High Bohemia," including "the Millionaire World, "especially those centering round feminism and sex-revolt" are symptoms of "Time"; as are technical achievements and commerce; art is "timeless."[41] What was being promoted as "daring" and "outrageous" art was in Lewis's view "mild," "tame," and "ridiculous," "nothing that would raise the pulse of a rabbit."[42] Related to this pseudo-revolution is the "cult of the child" expressed artistically in "the cult of the primitive and the savage," of Gauguin, for example.[43]

Democracy

Lewis's antipathy towards democracy is rooted in his theory of Time. He writes in *Men Without Art*, that democracy is hostile to artistic excellence and fosters "box office and library subscription standards."[44] Art, however, is timeless, classical. Democracy hates and victimizes the intellectual because the "mind" is aristocratic and offensive to the masses. Again, it is the dichotomy of the "romantic versus the classical." Conjoined with democracy is indus-

---

[39] Lewis, *Time and Western Man,* p. 42.

[40] Lewis, *Time and Western Man,* pp. 51–52.

[41] Lewis, *Time and Western Man,* p. 53.

[42] Lewis, *Time and Western Man,* p. 53.

[43] Lewis, *Time and Western Man,* p. 69.

[44] Wyndham Lewis, *Men Without Art* (London: Cassell, 1934), p. 263.

trialization, both representing the masses against the solitary genius. The result is the "herding of people into enormous mechanized masses." The "mass mind . . . is required to gravitate to a standard size to receive the standard idea."

Democracy and the advertisement are part and parcel of this debasement, and behind it all stands money, including the "millionaire bohemians" who control the arts. Making a romantic image of the machine, starting in Victorian times, is the product of our "Money-age." Vorticism, states Lewis, depicts the machine as befits an art that observes the Present, but unlike Futurism, does not idolize it. It is technology that generates change and revolution, but art remains constant; it is not in revolt against anything other than when society promotes conditions where art does not exist, as in democracy.

In Lewis's satirizing of the Bloomsbury denizens, he writes of the gulf between the elite and the masses, yet one that is not by necessity malevolent towards these masses:

> The intellect is more removed from the crowd than is anything: but it is not a snobbish withdrawal, but a going aside for the purposes of work, of work not without its utility for the crowd . . . More than the prophet or the religious teacher, [the leader] represents . . . the great unworldly element in the world, and that is the guarantee of his usefulness. And he should be relieved of the futile competition in all sorts of minor fields, so that his purest faculties could be free for the major tasks of intelligent creation.

Unfortunately, placing one's ideals onto the plane of activity results in vulgarization, a dilemma that caused Lewis's reservations towards Nietzsche. In *The Art of Being Ruled* Lewis writes that of every good thing, there comes its "shadow," "its ape and familiar." Lewis was still writing of this dilemma in *Rotting Hill* during the 1950s: "All the dilemmas of the creative seeking to function socially center upon the nature of action: upon the necessity of crude action, of calling in the barbarian to build a civilization."[45]

REVOLT OF THE PRIMITIVE

Lewis's book *Paleface: The Philosophy of the "Melting-Pot,"* inspired as a counter-blast to D. H. Lawrence, was written to repudiate the cult of the primitive—the Rousseauian ideal of the "return to nature" and of the "noble savage"—fashionable among the millionaire bohemians, as it had been among the parlor intellectuals of the eighteenth century. Although Lawrence was writing of primitive tribes to inspire a decadent European race to return to its own instinctual being, such "romanticism" is contrary to the classicism of Lewis, with its primacy of reason. Contrary to Lawrence, Lewis states that, "I would rather have an ounce of human consciousness than a universe full of 'abdominal' afflatus and hot, unconscious, 'soulless' mystical throbbing."[46]

In *Paleface* Lewis calls for a ruling caste of aesthetes, much like his friend Ezra Pound and his philosophical opposite Lawrence:

> We by birth the natural leaders of the white European, are people of no political or public consequence any more . . . We, the natural leaders in the World we live in, are now *private citizens* in the fullest sense, and that World is, as far as the administration of its traditional law of life is concerned, leaderless. Under these

[45] Wyndham Lewis, *Rotting Hill* (London: Methuen, 1951), p. 257.

[46] Wyndham Lewis, *Paleface: The Philosophy of the "Melting-Pot"* (New York: Haskell House, 1929), p. 196.

circumstances, its soul, in a generation or so, will be extinct.[47]

Lewis opposes the "melting pot" where different races and nationalities are becoming indistinguishable. Once again, Lewis's objections are aesthetic at their foundation. The Negro gift to the white man is jazz, "the aesthetic medium of a sort of frantic proletarian subconscious," degrading and exciting the masses into mindless energy, an "idiot mass sound" that is "Marxistic." We might reflect now that this was the beginning of the process upon which the modern music *industry* is largely founded, with "popular" music—the transient music of the mass market—centered around frenetic rhythms accompanied often by a frenzied pseudo-tribal dancing, symptomatic of the return the "cult of the primitive" in the name of "progress."

Compulsory Freedom

By the time Lewis wrote *Time and Western Man* he believed that people would have to be "compelled" to be free and individualistic. Reversing certain of his views espoused in *The Art of Being Ruled,* he now no longer believed that the urge of the masses to be enslaved should be organized, but rather that the masses will have to be compelled to be individualistic, writing: "I believe they could with advantage be compelled to remain absolutely alone for several hours every day; and a week's solitary confinement, under pleasant conditions (say in mountain scenery), every two months, would be an excellent provision. That and other coercive measures of a similar kind, I think, would make them much better people."[48]

One could argue that here again the process of industri-

---

[47] Lewis, *Paleface,* p. 82.

[48] Lewis, *Time and Western Man,* p. 138.

alization and the type of economic system that it entails, along with urbanization and the primacy of the city, are not conducive to anything other than the creation and sustaining of a frenzied, hurried mass on an economic treadmill. Every part of life is becoming subjected to the need for haste, even gastronomically in the form of "fast food" as the modern era's cuisine. The need for longer working hours proceeds contrary to the early expectations that the machine age would usher forth an era of more leisure during which the multitude would have time to reflect upon and even to create great art and literature, as per the utopian ideals of early socialist aesthetes such as William Morris and Oscar Wilde. Lewis's hope that individuals might one day be compelled to relax in solitude in order that they might become *real* individuals is further away than ever.

RETURN TO SOCIALIST ENGLAND

In 1939, Lewis and his wife went to the United States and on to Canada where Lewis lectured at Assumption College, a situation that did not cause discomfort, as he had long had a respect for Catholicism even though he was not a convert.

Lewis, the perpetual polemicist, began a campaign against extreme abstraction in art, attacking Jackson Pollock and the Abstract Expressionists.

He returned to England in 1945, and despite being completely blind by 1951, continued writing. In 1948, his *America and Cosmic Man* portrayed the US as the laboratory for a coming new world order of anonymity and utilitarianism. He saw the US as not a country but a "Cosmopolis."[49] He considered the American commitment not to national patriotism but to "brotherhood," because Americans are of

---

[49] Wyndham Lewis, *America and Cosmic Man* (New York: Country Life Press, 1949), p. 18.

"mixed race," and now to Lewis "brotherhood is a rather good thing to fight for,"[50] a combination of "puritan ethos and revolutionary politics . . ." a lesson to the world of "how to make the lion lay down with the lamb."[51]

As has been seen, Lewis paradoxically ridiculed Pound's belief in Social Credit but was also well aware of usury and the "Emperors of Debt." He considers this further in 1948 when writing:

> Monopolistic interests, with all the power such great interests dispose, set their face against any change in an antiquated system which has served their purpose so well, and which has so many advantages from their standpoint over a new model.
>
> The fairyland of bank capital and grandiose universal usury, out of which region a deep fog of unreality forever drifts overt into politics . . . is an Arcanum, of the very existence of which the average educated man is ignorant . . .
>
> All that need be said is that the great artificiality of politics, which in these pages I have been endeavoring to describe, is at least equaled, if not outdone, by the artificiality of economics. This is true of England as much as of America, though the United States is now the headquarters of world finance.[52]

Returning to England, Lewis received some "official" recognition when he was commissioned to write two dramas for BBC radio and became a regular columnist for *The Listener*.

A post-war poem, "If So the Man You Are," autobio-

---

[50] Lewis, *America and Cosmic Man*, p. 27.

[51] Lewis, *America and Cosmic Man*, pp. 30–31.

[52] Lewis, *America and Cosmic Man*, pp. 158–59.

graphically continues to reflect some of Lewis's abiding themes; that of the creative individual against the axis of the herd, of "High Finance, and Bolshevism":

The man I am to blow the bloody gaff
If I were given platforms? The riff-raff
May be handed all the trumpets that you will.
Not so the golden-tongued. The window-sill
Is all the pulpit they can hope to get.

What wind an honest mind advances? Look
No wind of sickle and hammer, of bell and book,
No wind of any party, or blowing out
Of any mountain blowing us about
Of "High Finance," or the foothills of same.
The man I am who does *not* play the game![53]

Lewis felt that "everything was drying up" in England, "extremism was eating at the arts, and the rot was pervasive in all levels of society." He writes of post-war England: "This is the capital of a dying empire—not crashing down in flames and smoke but expiring in a peculiar muffled way."

This is the England he portrays in his 1951 novel *Rotting Hill* (Ezra Pound's name for Notting Hill) where Lewis and his wife lived. The Welfare State symbolizes a shoddy utility standard in the pursuit of universal happiness. Socialist England causes everything to be substandard including shirt buttons that don't fit the holes, shoelaces too short to tie, scissors that won't cut, and inedible bread and jam. Lewis seeks to depict fully the socialist drabness of 1940s

---

[53] Wyndham Lewis, "If So the Man You Are," 1948, *The Penguin Book of Contemporary Verse* (Harmondsworth: Penguin Books, 1965), pp. 73–74.

Britain.

Unlike most of the literati who rebelled against Leftist dominance in the arts, Lewis came to uphold an ideal of a world culture overseen by a central world state, and a humanity that would become "Cosmic Man," seeing the US as the prototype of a future global society which the rest of the world would embrace.[54] He wrote his last novel *The Red Priest* in 1956. Lewis died in 1957, eulogized by T. S. Eliot in an obituary in the *Sunday Times*: "a great intellect has gone."

---

[54] Lewis, "Cosmic Society and Cosmic Man," in *America and Cosmic Man*.

CHAPTER 9

HENRY WILLIAMSON

HENRY WILLIAMSON, 1895–1977, was a member of the generation that fought the First World War, during which the experiences of the front gave rise to a new but eternal worldview. Williamson, like Knut Hamsun in Norway, saw man's place in nature as the ultimate source of our being—an idealization of nature as a reaction against the machine and the bank. His hope was of a new springtime for the West in Spenglerian terms. He was a partisan of the rural against the urban, rootedness in the soil and working the land against the nebulous city masses. It was what Spengler had called the final battle of civilization: "blood against money."[1]

Yet, while Williamson, Pound, and Hamsun were recognized for their crucial impact upon twentieth-century literature, they were consigned to oblivion for decades following the Second World War. This is because they not only identified with new political forms but also (unlike some of their contemporaries) never repudiated them. Williamson's outlook, shaped by both his experiences in the trenches and in his attachment to nature, led him to National Socialism, with its concept of "Blood and Soil,"[2] and to the distinctly

---

[1] The terms "blood" and "money" in the Spenglerian sense should be regarded as euphemisms for the *organic* and the *artificial* respectively. See Spengler, *The Decline of the West*, 2 vols., trans. Charles Francis Atkinson (London: George Allen and Unwin, 1971), vol. 2, pp. 506–507.

[2] For a scholarly account of the environmental and rural policies and ideology of the Third Reich see Anna Bramwell, *Blood and Soil: Richard Walther Darré and Hitler's "Green Party"* (Buckinghamshire: The Kensal Press, 1985).

British Fascism of Sir Oswald Mosley.

Williamson was born on December 1, 1895, in London, the son of a bank clerk. As a child, he had an intense love of nature, spending much of his time exploring the nearby Kent countryside. He was intent on closely observing things for himself, this faculty remaining with him throughout his life and providing the basis of his career as the author of famous and well-loved nature books.

World War I

Williamson enlisted in the army on the outbreak of the First World War and fought on the Somme and at Passchendaele, where he was seriously wounded. He was invalided home in 1915 but was back as an officer in France in 1916. He came out of the war as a captain with a Military Cross.

An enduring experience for Williamson was the Christmas Truce of 1914, when Germans and Englishmen left their trenches to fraternize and play soccer. Men such as Williamson returned from the war far from hating Germans and determined that never again would "brother Europeans" fight among themselves for the sake of greed and selfishness. The end of the war brought Williamson the numbing realization that the old world had died, and that such a war "must NEVER HAPPEN AGAIN."[3]

Man of the Soil

After demobilization, Williamson returned to his family home and entered employment with the *Weekly Dispatch* in Fleet Street. He had his first articles published in several major periodicals.

In 1919, he read *The Story of My Heart* by the nineteenth-century English nature writer Richard Jefferies. This was to

---

[3] Stephen Dorril, *Black Shirt: Sir Oswald Mosley and British Fascism* (London: Penguin Books, 2007), p. 33.

have a crucial impact upon Williamson as a revelation that he—the individual self—is more than an isolated echo but a link that stretches without beginning or end in a cosmic flow. Jefferies wrote of the rhythms of nature and of the soil, of seeking to reconnect with the earth, in a personal mystic union: "I see now that what I labored for was soul-life, more soul-nature. To be exalted, to be full of soul-learning. Finally I rose, walked half a mile or so along the summit of the hill eastwards, to soothe myself and come to the common ways of life again."[4]

Jefferies ends his idyllic vision of nature with a hope that the world, properly reorganized, will allow man the abundance of available resources without recourse to continuous labor; and that a system might develop that allows leisure time to create and to think, rather than to toil.[5] It was a problem that was to preoccupy many, from non-doctrinaire socialists of similar romantic bent, such as Oscar Wilde,[6] to Social Credit banking reformers, and was reflected in the agricultural policies of British Union and its post-war successor, the Union Movement.

Williamson returned to Jefferies in his autobiographical *Children of Shallowford,* where again he contemplates fraternization between Germans and British on Christmas Day, 1914 and states that, "Later still, I learned that one of the battalions mingling in comradeship with our volunteer battalion on that immortal day . . . was the List regiment, from Bavaria, in which served as Austrian volunteer named Adolf Hitler."

---

[4] Richard Jefferies, *The Story of My Heart: An Autobiography* (London: Longmans, Green, & Co., 1883), ch. 1.

[5] Jefferies, *The Story of My Heart,* ch. 11.

[6] Oscar Wilde, "The Soul of Man Under Socialism" (1891), in *The Complete Works of Oscar Wilde,* ed. Merlin Holland (London: HarperCollins, 2003).

Williamson takes down his "worn copy of Jefferies' *Story of My Heart*," reading from the writer he refers to as "a prophet crying in the industrial wilderness." The passages Williamson cites here from Jefferies refer to the desire to pass something better along to future generations, and to the transient, superficial character of "the piling up of fortunes, the building of cities, the establishment of immense commerce . . . these objects are so outside my idea that I cannot understand them, and look upon the struggle in amazement. . . . It is the human being, as the human being of whom I think . . ." Williamson remarks, "Richard Jefferies, the poor Wiltshire farmer's son, wrote that in 1875," ending with a tribute to Sir Oswald Mosley's British Union of Fascists as being the means by which these ideals might be accomplished:

> Illness, neglect, poverty—an early death—the usual fate of English men of genius. But Jefferies was not dead—he lived in the English flow of consciousness—he was immortal! He was with me, I was a trustee, in so far as my talents must be used, of the same ideas! . . . It was not until ten years later that I found, in British Union, an organization of men which was struggling to create a new world; and thereafter, I was among friends.[7]

In 1921 Williams embarked on *The Beautiful Years*, the first volume of the four-volume *Flax of Dreams*. In 1922, Williamson returned to the countryside and rented a cottage that had been built in the days of King John, next to the local church in Georgeham, North Devon. Williamson lived here hermit-like and studied nature in detail, tramp-

---

[7] Henry Williamson, "Autobiography," from *The Children of Shallowford*, in *Selections from BUF Quarterly*, ed. E. R. Fields (Marietta, Ga.: The Truth at Last, 1995), pp. 59–64.

ing the countryside and sleeping out. The doors and windows of his cottage were always open, and he gathered about him a family of dogs, cats, gulls, buzzards, magpies, and an otter cub.

Williamson had rescued the otter after a farmer had shot its mother. He named him Tarka (meaning little water wanderer). The otter would walk like a dog alongside Williamson. One day Tarka walked into a rabbit trap, panicked, and fled. Williamson spent years looking for Tarka, following the rivers Taw and Torridge. He didn't find the otter, but he was inspired to write his most famous nature book, *Tarka the Otter*. Published in 1927, this popular book was an intimate description of the English countryside and gained Williamson the Hawthorne Prize for Literature in 1928.

In 1925, Williamson married, and his first son was born the following year. In 1929, the family moved to Shallowford, Devon, where over the next thirteen years four more children were sired, and more books were published, including *Salar the Salmon*. From 1937–45 the Williamson family lived at the Old Hall Farm in North Norfolk, where many more books and articles were written, and a sixth child was born.

National Socialism

Like Sir Oswald Mosley and the many veterans who joined his British Union of Fascists, Williamson was appalled by the prospect of another war that would again soak the fields of Europe with the blood of closely-related peoples. Not only had the fraternity of the front on Christmas, 1914 forever affected him, but he was also greatly influenced by the act of the German officer who had helped him remove a wounded British soldier caught in barbed wire on the front line. On another occasion, Williamson had heard the weak cry of a German lad wounded on the battlefield, who in delirium was calling for his mother. Williamson assuring the boy that his mother was there. In spite of the particular horror of World War I, it is probably the last major war that retained a vestige of the Western chivalric ethos.

Jeffrey Hamm, Mosley's principal post-World War II aide, reflecting on Williamson and the other veterans who joined Mosley, writes:

> There were the soldiers who had been assured by the old men of the Establishment that they would return to "a land fit for heroes," only to find that they had been cheated and betrayed. The returning ex-serviceman was thrown on to the scrap-heap of unemployment, and officers joined with the men they had commanded in selling matches and bootlaces in the streets of an ungrateful country. In bitterness and cynicism that the promised "land fit for heroes" had become one in which you had to be a hero to survive. In later years many of them turned to Fascism, in Britain and all over Europe.[8]

Williamson was therefore able to contrast what he knew of the chivalry of the Germans with the anti-German propaganda that the press had begun to resurrect with the advent of Hitler.[9] In 1930 he revisited Ypres and wrote *The Patriot's Progress,* the story of a bank clerk invalided home who came to realize that the war was a "dirty trick" played on the younger generation by the older and was responsi-

---

[8] Jeffrey Hamm, *Action Replay* (London: Howard Baker, 1983), pp. 18–19.

[9] "Atrocity propaganda" had been used to good effect by the British during World War I, with tales of German soldiers throwing babies into the air as part of bayonet practice, and the like.

ble for "most, if not everything, that was wrong with England."[10]

Williamson saw in National Socialism a spirit that could bring a dying Western civilization back to the wellspring of its life. He felt duty-bound to raise a voice. He was one of the first to commit himself to Mosley and the British Union of Fascists, although he did not join the British Union until 1937.[11] He championed Hitler as the visionary leader of European rebirth. In *The Flax of Dreams* and *The Phoenix Generation* Williamson was to describe Hitler as "the great man across the Rhine whose life symbol is the happy child." Another war against Germany would only serve "Oriental commissars" waiting "like jackals to grow fat on the killings."[12]

THE BRITISH UNION OF FASCISTS

Williamson saw in Mosley's British Union of Fascists the movement most committed to agriculture and the country. Mosley, clearly influenced by the ideas of Oswald Spengler, warned in a speech that, "the roots of Britain are being dragged from the soil. . . . Any civilization that is to endure requires constant replenishment from the steady, virile stock which is bred in the health, sanity, and natural but arduous labour of the countryside."[13]

British Union propagandist A. K. Chesterton wrote that, "unless they know, mystically, that beneath the concrete lies the earth which has nourished their race for a thousand years and . . . that it is their own earth from which their

---

[10] Henry Williamson, *The Patriot's Progress* (1930) (London: Macdonald, 1968).

[11] Roger Eatwell, *Fascism: A History* (London: Vintage, 1996), p. 188.

[12] Henry Williamson, *The Phoenix Generation* (London: Macdonald, 1965), p. 349.

[13] Dorril, *Black Shirt*, p. 417.

blood is shed and renewed, then they are a lost people, and easy prey for those who have lacked roots for many centuries."[14]

Francis McEvoy, writing in *BUF Quarterly*, expressed nostalgia for the country he had known, addressing himself to the "peasant folk of Britain" who had been driven off the land, to the cities by the "blighting tyranny of modern capitalism." Summoning his own experiences, McEvoy, somewhat reminiscent of Hamsun, referred to the simplicity of life and the rhythm of the seasons of which country folk are a part, only asking for a modest return to "live on the land of our fathers."

Food imports were destroying British agriculture as part of a system that "crowds the people of Britain into offices and factories," subjecting the dwellers of the great cities to "economic servitude." This was leading to human standardization in the pursuit of "greed, materialism, triviality" and exploitation: "Long live the 'little man,' standardized like a mass-produced motor car, the swarm of Babbitts from the service flats and the suburbs, propagandized, exploited, and brutified, in 'this England of ours'! . . . The death of the countryside portends the death of the nation, for from the soil springs all life, physical and spiritual."[15]

Mosley's agricultural adviser was New Zealand-born Jorian Jenks, who had been driven from his own farm because of the Slump. Jenks was a pioneer of organic farming. He had held government appointments as an agricultural specialist, and he was an organizer of the Rural Reconstruction Association.

With a commitment not only to a rural revival, but also

---

[14] Dorril, *Black Shirt*, p. 417.

[15] Francis McEvoy, "The Disinherited of the Soil," in *Selections from BUF Quarterly*, pp. 22–23.

to sincerely pursuing peace,[16] the British Union of Fascists, together with the qualities of courage and intelligence that Williamson saw in Mosley, had everything to commend it. He stated of Mosley in relation to his own commitment to rural life, "The spirit of the farm and what I was trying to do there was the spirit of Oswald Mosley. It was all part of the same battle."[17]

The great personal commitment that Williamson had to Mosley is expressed in *The Phoenix Generation*, the twelfth volume of his post-World War II, semi-autobiographical fifteen-volume saga *Chronicle of Ancient Sunlight*, where Mosley is portrayed by the character Sir Hereward Birkin, who opposed international finance, the "Minotaur which claims another generation of European youth to bleed to death on the battlefields":

> Birkin is *my* generation, he is English of the English. I think it a great pity that he resigned from the Labour party. But then all history is a pity. He belonged to the war generation, and we survivors all resolved to *do something*, to *be* something different when it was all over on the Western Front, that great livid wound that lay across Europe suppurating during more than fifteen hundred nights and days—torrents of steel and prairie fires of flame, the roar of creation if you like. Birkin should have remained in Parliament—that was his platform, but what's the use of talking about

---

[16] Unlike certain other forms of Fascism outside Britain, and the views of other veteran literati such as Ernst Jünger in Germany, and Marinetti in Italy, who declared "war is the world's hygiene," Mosley and his variety of "British Fascism" did not hold any romantic ideals about war.

[17] Quoted in *Radio Times*, August 17, 1972; cited by Robert Skidelsky, *Oswald Mosley* (London: Macmillan, 1975), p. 350.

> should-haves, or might-haves? Birkin remains the only man of prominence in England with the new spirit. He limped away from the battlefield determined that never again would it happen. Perhaps such a spirit can only be acceptable to a new generation after another war. When he is dead. And I hope I'll be dead too.[18]

In *The Solitary War,* the thirteenth volume of *Chronicle of Ancient Sunlight,* Williamson's semi-autobiographical character Philip Maddison states that Hitler

> freed the farmers from the mortgages which drained the land, cleared the slums, inspired work for all the seven million unemployed, got them to believe in their greatness, each one a German to do his utmost in whatever was his work—in the *Arbeitsdienst* draining swamp land or making Europe's new autobahn, stripped to the waist—the former pallid leer of hopeless slum youth transformed into the sun-tan, the clear eye, the broad and easy rhythm of the poised young human being.[19]

Lest it be objected that Williamson was seeing Germany through rose-colored glasses, very much the same description was given in the perennially-published anti-Nazi primer *The Rise and Fall of the Third Reich,* by the American journalist William L. Shirer, whose hatred of Hitler is beyond doubt:

> The young in the Third Reich were growing up to

---

[18] Williamson, *The Phoenix Generation,* p. 349.

[19] Henry Williamson, *The Solitary War* (London: Macdonald, 1966), p. 365.

> have strong and healthy bodies, faith in the future of their country and in themselves, and a sense of fellowship and camaraderie that shattered all class and economic and social barriers. I thought of that later, in the May days of 1940, when along the road between Aachen and Brussels one saw the contrasts between the German soldiers, bronzed and clean cut from a youth spent in the sunshine on an adequate diet, and the first British war prisoners, with their hollow chests, round shoulders, pasty complexions and bad teeth—tragic examples of the youth that England had neglected so irresponsibly in the years between the wars.[20]

Williamson attended the 1935 Nuremberg Congress with Mosley's sister-in-law Unity Mitford, an avid Hitlerite. He was impressed by the economic and social achievements of Germany while the British continued to languish in poverty and unemployment. He saw a racial community based on the values of land and a revived peasantry, freed from banker's interest, guaranteed from foreclosure, and supported by pioneering conservation laws and projects. Williamson saw in the faces of the German people an expressiveness and confidence that looked as if they were "breathing extra oxygen," as he put it. He wrote of the SA Brownshirts as having "the spirit of English gentlemen who had transcended class consciousness."[21]

Through the war Williamson was still getting published,

---

[20] William L. Shirer, *The Rise and Fall of the Third Reich: A History of Nazi Germany* (New York: Book Club Associates, 1977), p. 256.

[21] David Pryce-Jones, *Unity Mitford: A Quest* (London: W. H. Allen, 1978), p. 141.

despite the polemical nature of his books. The locals at Stiffkey, Norfolk, aware of his pro-German attitudes, suspected that he was a spy sending signals to the enemy. He was detained for a weekend in June 1940 under Regulation 18B.[22]

In *The Story of a Norfolk Farm*, published in 1941, describing the life on the 250-acre farm he had purchased in 1937, Williamson writes in thoroughly "fascist," completely subversive mode, placing political parties and the financial and economic system on par with rats, weeds, swamps, and pollution:

> Rats, weeds, swamps, depressed markets, labourers on the dole, rotten cottages, polluted streams, political parties and class divisions controlled by the money power, wealthy banking and insurance houses getting rid of their land mortgages and investing their millions abroad (but not in the empire), this was the real England of the period of this story of a Norfolk farm . . .
>
> . . . One day the sewage of the cities will cease to be poured into the rivers, and will be returned to the land, to grow fine food for the people. One day salmon will leap again in the clear waters of the London River; and human work will be creative and joyful.
>
> One day the soul of man, shut in upon itself during the long centuries of economic struggle, will arise in the light of the sun of truth. And now I lay down the pen and return to the plough.[23]

---

[22] The Henry Williamson Society, "The Norfolk Farm," http://www.henrywilliamson.co.uk/index.php?option=com_content&view=article&id=71&Itemid=102

[23] Henry Williamson, *The Story of a Norfolk Farm* (London: Faber & Faber, 1941).

Williamson maintained these themes with no less determination after the war, writing similarly in *The Phoenix Generation,* through the semi-autobiographical Philip Maddison:

> When the soil's fertility is being conserved instead of raped, when village life is a social unity, when pride of craftsmanship returns, when everyone works for the sake of adding beauty and importance to life, when every river is clean and bright, and the proud words "I serve" are in everyone's heart and purpose. Then my country will be good enough for me.[24]

PEACE WORK

As noted previously, one of Williamson's primary political motivations was preventing another war. He called for Anglo-German brotherhood, recognizing that Hitler desired nothing more than peace with Britain. He sought to have his friend T. E. Lawrence (of Arabia) join with Mosley in a peace campaign. According to Williamson, Lawrence considered Hitler to be a humble servant of his people, who was being misrepresented by the press.

Of this account, Lawrence, like Williamson, believed that peace could be maintained by the actions of the ex-servicemen of Britain and Germany: "The English ex-Service man respected the German ex-Service man; and the German ex-Servicemen were in power in Germany." In Williamson's peace plan, Lawrence would call a mass meeting of ex-Servicemen in the Albert Hall, London, which would have an impact upon the ex-servicemen of Britain, Germany, and France because of Lawrence's prestige.

Again, Williamson harks back to Christmas Day, 1914,

---

[24] Williamson, *The Phoenix Generation,* p. 349.

when Germans and British troops fraternized in no-man's land, and the Establishment panicked lest peace spontaneously break out *en masse*. This event had always remained the basis of Williamson's hope for an accord in Europe. Williamson wrote of Lawrence: "I believe that had he lived, Lawrence would have confirmed the inner hopes of every ex-Service man in Europe: that the Spirit of Christmas Day, 1914 . . . already hovering in the air, would have swiftly materialised and given, generally in Europe, a vision of a new conception of life."[25] Lawrence died in a motorcycle accident, which some believe suspicious, on returning from having mailed an answer to Williamson's appeal that he should meet Hitler. Lawrence sought to discuss the matter with Williamson without delay.[26]

With Mosley's rallies attracting larger audiences than ever in 1940, Williamson wrote to Mosley: "If I could see him [Hitler], as a common soldier who had fraternized, on the faraway Christmas Day of 1914, with the men of his Linz battalion under Messines Hill, might I not be able to give him the amity he so desired from England, a country he admired . . . ?"[27] Williamson visited Mosley full of hope, but Mosley's reaction was that "I am afraid the curtain is down." Williamson nodded and asked Mosley what he would do. Mosley replied that he would carry on as long as possible working for peace.[28]

In 1940, around a thousand Englishmen were interned without trial for opposing the war, including Mosley and

---

[25] Henry Williamson, "Lawrence of Arabia and Germany," *Anglo-German Review*, January 1937, p. 107.

[26] Henry Williamson, in *T. E. Lawrence by His Friends*, ed. A. W. Lawrence (London: Jonathan Cape, 1937).

[27] Skidelsky, *Oswald Mosley*, p. 442.

[28] Skidelsky, *Oswald Mosley*, pp. 442–43.

over 700 BUF members.[29] As noted previously Williamson was jailed for a weekend on suspicion of being a "spy." Williamson was released on condition that he remain silent, a condition that he managed to circumvent, as we have seen from his novels during the war years. With the defeat of Germany, Williamson stated that his hopes for a regenerated Europe had been killed.

The Gale of the World

Williamson's first marriage broke up in 1947. He returned to North Devon to live in the hilltop hut he had bought in 1928. In *The Gale of the World*,[30] the last volume of his 15 volume *Chronicle of Ancient Sunlight*, Williamson has Philip Maddison (i.e., himself) questioning the legality of the Nuremberg Trials and the devastation of Germany, and puts the blame for the mass deaths in German concentration camps partly on the Allied bombing of the German transport system.

Williamson remained loyal to Sir Oswald Mosley (the character Sir Hereward Birkin in *The Gale of the World*). In this last volume, he has Maddison write some notes for guidance to a young writer, a survivor of the Second World War who aspires to write a *War and Peace* for this age. Williamson asks hopefully whether such a writer might write from his own spirit and vision, "unimpeded and unimpaired by contemporary massed emotions to truly show the luminous personality of Adolf Hitler": to write with "divination and truth, without admiration or contempt, and above all without moral judgment, of the causes and effects of the tragic split in the mind of European man, from which arose this war."

---

[29] Skidelsky, *Oswald Mosley*, p. 449.

[30] Henry Williamson, *The Gale of the World* (London: Macdonald, 1969).

The creator of a work of art, continues Williamson/Maddison, will reveal the truth of this age, "holding in balance the forces and counter-forces which led to the disintegration of the West." "The mind of the poet must with detachment assess the fatal war with an "admired sister nation," which resulted in exposing the West to "a greater ruin from the East," because a leader (Churchill) pursued Britain's centuries-old policy of European "balance of power" and thereby endorsed the further decline of the West by destroying Germany.

Williamson/Maddison, questions whether there was a soul of Britain or just a "disruptive determination," arising from its island isolation and its position of wealth from trade. "Its policy for four hundred years has been to rule by money, thus keeping in division the continent of Europe," as Winston Churchill has written in an early autobiography: "And will history decide that this European of great talent and emotion [Churchill] felt it to be his crowning purpose in life to balk and destroy a fellow European [Hitler] of genius—who could build only because he had forced out money for money's sake?"[31]

It had been a war of the "spiritually damaged." The German leadership was being tried and executed unchivalrously for war crimes, when the Soviets had been guilty of Katyn. When thousands of shopkeepers in France were murdered and their shops looted, they were condemned as "collaborators."

Early in *The Gale of the World,* Maddison notes that after Berlin had been subdued by the shelling from 11,000 guns,

> rape and sadism preceded slow murder. Neither those "war criminals" nor their Russian Generals are being tried at Nuremberg.

---

[31] Williamson, *The Gale of the World,* p. 171.

> What of the so-called Allied war crimes? We are impotent to do anything about the loss of Poland's integrity. What the war was about for Churchill, and those who sought to keep Europe down and divided, was the preventing of Hitler from making Europe united and self-sufficient, and independent of loans and imports.
>
> For this is what the war was about; it was not directly about Synagogues burned down or heads shaved or Catholics saying Mass or anything else which the man in the street was told, since that was ALL he could comprehend. The war, was, and remains, an economic war; and historically speaking, the misery of generations is less in eternity than a wave expending itself on a rock. The European wave breaks, and is no more.[32]

Williamson has a doctor attached to the dispossessed Ukrainians in Britain point out that Hitler ordered the German tanks to halt at Dunkirk: "Declaring that he had no quarrel with the English, and wished not to invade or injure in anyway a 'cousin nation,' the Führer said that if the British Empire went down, the Germans, although they would win the war in Europe, would go down under Bolshevism. Because we did not command the sea as well."[33] Williamson was acutely aware that the Soviets had been permitted to invade half of Europe while the British and American forces were held back, and that they would soon have the atomic bomb.

Maddison notes on the radio news the final words of the defendants at Nuremberg as they went to their deaths on the scaffold. Immediately he makes a note: "Hermann Gö-

---

[32] Williamson, *The Gale of the World*, p. 27.

[33] Williamson, *The Gale of the World*, p. 66.

ring shot down Manfred Cloudesley over Mossy Face Wood at Havrincourt in 1918. He saw that his enemy, who had killed nine of his Richtofen Staffel pilots, had the best surgeons and treatment in hospital. This morning Göring committed suicide, better to have died on the cross, old Knight of the Order Pour le Mérite."[34]

POST-WAR & OSWALD MOSLEY

In *The Gale of the World,* Williamson picks up with Mosley's post-war campaign, stating of Mosley (Sir Hereward Birkin): "Many perceptive men recognized him as a young man of outstanding brilliance, industry and courage. Now let the author of this book speak for himself." Williamson then quotes from Mosley's post-war manifesto, *The Alternative*:

> We were divided and we are conquered. That is the tragic epitaph of two war generations. That was the fate of my generation in 1914, and that was the doom of a new generation of young soldiers in 1939. The youth of Europe shed the blood of their own family, and the jackals of the world grew fat. Those who fought are in the position of the conquered, whatever their country. Those who did not fight, but merely profited, alone are victorious.[35]

Williamson takes up Mosley's post-war analysis, stating that Fascism had failed because it was too national. Its opponent, financial democracy, failed too. "It could only frustrate those who would build a New Order." There follows a long excerpt from *The Alternative,* ending with a call for

---

[34] Williamson, *The Gale of the World,* p. 98.

[35] Oswald Mosley, *The Alternative* (Ramsbury: Mosley Publications, 1947).

Europeans to overcome their old wounds and rivalries and march onward in the "European Spirit."

Williamson was one of the first to respond to Mosley's post-war call for a United Europe and wrote for the new magazine of Mosley's Union Movement, *The European*, in which he proclaimed the birth of a new Europe in tune with nature. The journal, despite the "notoriety" of its founder, Mosley, attracted many eminent writers. Ezra Pound kept his faith in Mosley, and his poems appeared in *The European*.[36] Williamson contributed his reminiscences of the poet Roy Campbell.[37]

Under the direction of Jorian Jenks, the post-war Union Movement continued to advocate the renewal of agriculture, demanding self-sufficiency in food, fair prices, and a regulated market, a corporative or syndicalist representation of farmers, farm workers, and consumers to administer agriculture production and distribution, credit for agricultural development, a preference for organic methods, and "a vigorous land policy, reserving all fertile land for food production, fostering land settlement, promoting the improvement and repopulation of marginal and hill lands, and insisting on high standards of husbandry with special emphasis on soil fertility."[38]

Like Ezra Pound and Knut Hamsun, Williamson was denied honors and ignored for decades. Mosley's post-war aide, Jeffrey Hamm, writing of his "old friend" Williamson, stated that:

---

36 Ezra Pound, "Ci de los Cantares," *The European*, vol. 12, no. 6, February 1959, pp. 382–84.

37 Henry Williamson, "Roy Campbell: A Portrait," *The European*, vol. 12, no. 6, February 1959, pp. 357–58.

38 Jorian Jenks, *None Need Starve*, Union Movement Agricultural Council (London: Robert Row, 1952).

> After the war, when he was creating, as many thought, his masterpiece, the fifteen-volume novel known collectively as *A Chronicle of Ancient Sunlight*, his books frequently received dismissive reviews, or none at all. The degrees committee of the university of which he was a signal benefactor twice vetoed the proposal to award him an honorary doctorate. In spite of representations made, unknown to him, by friends and admirers, his name was not put forward for recognition in New Year or Birthday honours' lists.[39]

Richard Thurlow opines that

> Indeed it is his support for Mosley, expressed on many occasions, which goes some way to account for the continuing neglect of his work by much of the literary establishment. Even the most perceptive of critics of the literature of the First World War, Paul Fussell, has totally ignored Williamson's most important work on this theme. This is indeed unfortunate, for Williamson, perhaps more than any other writer, accurately described the experience of the common man in the trenches and the lingering and traumatic effects it had on the survivors of the experience.[40]

In 1950 Williamson remarried and sired another son, divorcing in 1968. His *Chronicle of Ancient Sunlight* was written between 1951 and 1969, and was acclaimed as a masterpiece of English literature, despite the efforts of certain

---

[39] Hamm, *Action Replay*, p. 226.

[40] Richard Thurlow, *British Fascism: A History, 1918–1985* (Oxford: Basil Blackwell, 1987), p. 26.

interests to obliterate his name. In 1972, he published his final book *The Scandaroon*, the story of a racing pigeon. In 1974, he began working on the script for a film of *Tarka*. Unknown to Williamson, filming went ahead despite the failing health that prevented him from completing the task himself. Williamson died on August 13, 1977, and was buried in North Devon. Mosley said that Williamson had always remained his "great friend."[41]

---

[41] Oswald Mosley, *My Life* (London: Nelson, 1968), p. 226.

CHAPTER 10

ROY CAMPBELL

ROY CAMPBELL, 1901–1957, was born in the Natal District of South Africa. He enjoyed an idyllic childhood, imbued as much with Zulu traditions and language as with his Scottish heritage.[1] He showed early talent as an artist, but an interest in literature including poetry soon became predominant.[2]

In 1918 he travelled to England to attend Oxford. By this time he was an agnostic with a love for Elizabethan literature.[3] Campbell's friendship with the composer William Walton at Oxford brought him into contact with such literati as T. S. Eliot, the Sitwells, and Wyndham Lewis.[4] He was by now reading Freud, Darwin, and Nietzsche.[5] He had a distaste for Anglo-Saxonism and the "drabness of England" but found an affinity with the Celts.[6] Campbell identified with the Futurists, but his views are suggestive of the classicism of T. E. Hulme. He also became attached to the Vorticist movement of Ezra Pound and Wyndham Lewis:

> Art is not developed by a lot of long-haired fools in velvet jackets. It develops itself and pulls those fools wherever it wants them to go . . . Futurism is the reac-

---

1 Joseph Pearce, *Bloomsbury and Beyond: The Friends and Enemies of Roy Campbell* (London: HarperCollins, 2001), pp. 1–2.

2 Pearce, *Bloomsbury and Beyond,* p. 9.

3 Pearce, *Bloomsbury and Beyond,* p. 23.

4 Pearce, *Bloomsbury and Beyond,* p. 22.

5 Pearce, *Bloomsbury and Beyond,* p. 30.

6 Pearce, *Bloomsbury and Beyond,* p. 44.

> tion caused by the faintness, the morbid wistfulness of the symbolists. It is hard, cruel, and glaring, but always robust and healthy.
>
> It is art pulling itself together for another tremendous fight against annihilation. It is wild, distorted, and ugly, like a wrestler coming back for a last tussle against his opponent. The muscles are contorted and rugged, the eyes bulge, and the legs stagger. But there it is, and it has won the victory.[7]

Campbell escaped from England's "drabness" to Provence where he worked on fishing boats and picked grapes. Despite his agnosticism, he was impressed by the simple faith of the peasants and the fishermen with whom he worked, and started writing poems of a religious nature such as *Saint Peter of the Three Canals – The Fisher's Prayer,* which took ten years—beginning in 1920—to complete, and portrays Campbell's spiritual odyssey. He returned to London in 1921, married Mary Garman, and became highly regarded among the Bloomsbury coterie, who were impressed with his rough manners and hard drinking.

His wife inspired his first epic poem *The Flaming Terrapin,* written while the couple lived for over a year in a remote Welsh village where their first daughter was born. T. E. Lawrence was immediately impressed with the poem and took it to Jonathan Cape for publication.[8] This established Campbell's reputation as a poet.

NIETZSCHE, CHRIST, & THE HEROIC POET

The Flaming Terrapin is a combination of Christianity and

---

[7] Roy Campbell, *Light on a Dark Horse: An Autobiography, 1901–1935* (London: Hollis and Carter, 1951), p. 230.

[8] Peter Alexander, *Roy Campbell: A Critical Biography* (Oxford: Oxford University Press, 1982), p. 34.

Nietzsche. In a letter to his parents, Campbell sought to explain the symbolism as being founded on Christ's statements: "Every tree that bringeth not forth good fruit is hewn down, and cast into the fire" (Matthew 7: 19) and "Ye are the salt of the earth: but if that salt shall have lost its savor, wherewith shall it be salted? It is henceforth good for nothing, but to be cast out, and to be trodden under foot of men" (Matthew 5: 13).

Campbell now realized that Christ was the first to "proclaim the doctrine of heredity and survival of the fittest," and that his "aristocratic outlook" was misunderstood by Nietzsche as being a religion of the weak. World War I had destroyed the best breeding stock and demoralized humanity. The Russians, for example, had succumbed to Bolshevism. But Campbell hoped that a portion might become ennobled from the suffering.[9]

He continued to explain that the deluge in *The Flaming Terrapin* represents the World War and that Noah's family represents "the survival of the fittest," triumphing over the terrors of the storm to colonize the earth. The terrapin in Eastern tradition is the tortoise that represents "strength, longevity, endurance, and courage" and is the symbol of the universe. It is this "flaming terrapin" that tows the Ark, and wherever he crawls upon the earth, creation blossoms forth. He is "masculine energy," and where his voice roars man springs forth from the soil. His acts of creation are born from "action and flesh in one clean fusion."[10]

The poem, published in 1924 in Britain and the United States, received critical acclaim from the press as a fresh and youthful breath, as breaking free from both the banalities of the past and from the skeptical nihilism of the new generation.

---

[9] Pearce, *Bloomsbury and Beyond*, pp. 50–51.

[10] Pearce, *Bloomsbury and Beyond*, pp. 51–52.

Campbell and his family returned to South Africa where he was welcomed as a celebrity. Campbell lectured on Nietzsche, praising Nietzsche's condemnation of the meanness of modern democracy.[11] He also started expressing a lifelong neo-Luddite attitude to technology:

> Our progress in mechanical science during the last century has so far outpaced the development of our intellectual and moral faculties that we have suddenly lost ourselves. All those useful mechanical toys which man primarily invented for his own convenience have begun to tyrannize every moment of his life . . .[12]

This was a theme that concerned Campbell throughout his life. In a poem written a year later entitled "The Serf," Campbell proclaimed the tiller of the soil as "timeless" as he "ploughs down palaces, and thrones, and towers." The tiller of the soil, states a hopeful Campbell, endures through eternity while the cycles of history rise and fall around him. This gives a sense of permanence in a constantly shifting world. It is a theme shared by other literati of the time, in particular Knut Hamsun and Henry Williamson.

---

[11] Pearce, *Bloomsbury and Beyond*, p. 60.

[12] Pearce, *Bloomsbury and Beyond*, p. 60. This is a problem that was also at the forefront of Nobel Laureate Dr. Alexis Carrel's concern, Carrel also turning to the "Right" in recognition of the need for tradition and religion. See K. R. Bolton, *Alexis Carrel: A Commemoration* (Paraparaumu Beach, New Zealand: Renaissance Press, 2010). Jung held the view that there are levels of man's psyche that are still not finished with the primeval and the medieval, yet that are suddenly thrust into the technological era, causing psychological fragmentation. See C. G. Jung, *Memories, Dreams, Reflections*, ed. Aniela Jaffé, trans. Richard and Clara Winston (New York: Pantheon, 1961), p. 263.

His poem in honor of his wife, "Dedication to Mary Campbell," is Nietzschean in theme but also a criticism of his fellow South Africans, referring to the poet as "living by sterner laws," as not concerned with their commerce, and as worshipping a god "superbly stronger than their own."

ESTRANGED FROM SOUTH AFRICANS

In 1925 Campbell became editor of *Voorslag*[13] and was closely associated with William Plomer whose first novel, *Turbott Wolfe*, involves interracial marriage. However, despite their friendship and Campbell's disdain for the racial situation in South Africa, he reviewed Plomer's novel and found it to have "a very strong bias against the white colonists." Nevertheless, Campbell was not impressed by what he considered as white South Africa, "reclining blissfully in a grocer's paradise on the labor of the natives."[14]

Some of Campbell's poems written in South Africa at this time are considered to be among his best. "To a Pet Cobra" returns to Nietzschean themes, describing poets in heroic terms, the Zarathustrian solitary atop the mountain peaks:

There shines upon the topmost peak of peril
There is not joy like them who fight alone
And in their solitude a tower of pride

BLOOMSBURY & PROVENCE

On their return to Britain, Campbell and his wife were introduced to the Bloomsbury coterie, including the poet-

---

[13] Campbell resigned from the editorship of *Voorslag* after the publisher's interference.

[14] Roy Campbell, *Voorslag*, vol. 1, no. 1, June 1926, in Roy Campbell, *Collected Works*, vol. 4: Prose (Craighall, South Africa: Ad. Donker, 1985), pp. 195–96.

ess Vita Sackville-West, her husband the novelist Harold Nicolson, Virginia and Leonard Woolf, Richard Aldington, Aldous Huxley, Lytton Strachey, *et al.* The robust Campbell found their refined manners, pervasive homosexuality, and pretentiousness sickening, writing in "Home Thoughts on Bloomsbury" that his own voice is the only one he likes to hear when around all the "clever people."[15]

It is little wonder that Campbell found such an affinity with the fierce critic of Bloomsbury, Wyndham Lewis, becoming Lewis' militant defender when Bloomsbury savaged him. Several years later in *The Georgiad,* Campbell satirizes the dinner parties of Bloomsbury where, wishing to stop the "din" in his "dizzy" head, he imagines stuffing his ears with fish and bread, and wishes the diners would choke on their food so that their chattering would cease.[16]

To septuagenarian Peter-Pans,
To Bloomsburies, to Fabians, to Sissies,
To swotters-up of philosophic blisses,
To busybodies of the wagging tongue
And all whose follies have remained unsung,
Some of whom are good fellows, I admit,
And gain in niceness what they lack in wit:
But whose collective dictatorial rule
Would wake the devil in the tamest mule . . .

. . . Our whole identity into one same
Class, sex, community, where even name
And all distinctions in the dust shall slumber . . .

---

[15] Roy Campbell, "Home Thoughts on Bloomsbury," *Collected Works,* vol. 1 (Craighall, South Africa: Ad. Donker, 1985), p. 196.

[16] Roy Campbell, "The Georgiad," Part Three, *Collected Works,* vol. 1, p. 207.

. . . When prudery, anonymity, and chat
Have killed all difference between this and that . . .[17]

In 1928 the Campbells returned to Provence. The atmosphere was altogether different from England's wealthy socialist intelligentsia, from whom he sought escape. The Campbells fully involved themselves in the community, celebrated the harvest feasts, and welcomed the local folk into their home. Campbell became a celebrated figure in the dangerous sport of "water jousting."[18] He also assisted in the ring at bullfights. In the customs and culture of the Provençal villagers, he found a stability and permanence in a changing world obsessed by science and "progress." His own aesthetics, at the basis of his rejection of liberalism and socialism, was a synthesis of the romanticism of Provence and the classicism of the Greco-Romans. He admired Caesar and the stoicism and martial ethos of the ancients. His ideal was a combination of aesthete and athlete.

In *Taurine Provence*, which his publisher described as the "philosophy, technique, and religion of the bullfighter,"[19] Campbell writes of this: "So men in whom the heroic principle works will be driven by their very excess of vitality to flaunt their defiance in the face of death or danger, as in the modern arena."[20]

Campbell, freed from the English intelligentsia, now renewed his attack with fury. In an essay on contemporary poetry published in *Scrutinies*, he states that the dominant philosophy of the contemporary writer is dictated more by

---

[17] Campbell, "The Georgiad," Part Three, *Collected Works*, vol. 1, p. 216.

[18] Pearce, *Bloomsbury and Beyond*, p. 109.

[19] Alexander, *Roy Campbell*, p. 121.

[20] Roy Campbell, *Taurine Provence* (London: Desmond Harmsworth, 1932).

"fear of discomfort, excitement, or pain than by love of life."[21] His attack on the "sex-socialism" of Bloomsbury as being flabby and effete is contrasted with his own robust nature that could not fit in with the simpering and decadent atmosphere of the intellectual salon.

Following on from Wyndham Lewis' scathing attack on Bloomsbury, *The Apes of God,* which Campbell enjoyed immensely, Campbell wrote his own broadside, *The Georgiad.* This would bring down on him the same mixture of condemnation and silence that the intellectual coterie had used against Wyndham Lewis.

Not surprisingly, Campbell relished being Lewis' literary "bodyguard." After the Bloomsbury literary boycott in response to *The Apes of God,* Campbell wrote "Wyndham Lewis: An Essay," but this too was boycotted and was not published until recently. In this essay, Campbell sets out to explain and defend the key polemical positions of Lewis' books. He describes Lewis' *Paleface,* an attack on D. H. Lawrence's revival of the "cult of the primitive," as "scrupulously fair," Lewis and Campbell considering Lawrence to have launched a literary attack on "the consciousness of the European white, [which] exalts the blind tom-tom beating instincts of the savage."[22] *Paleface* moreover should be read in conjunction with Lewis' book *Hitler,* where Lewis shows that the "racial solution of Hitlerism should not entirely be despised (if not necessarily to be swallowed whole)," whereas the revival of the utopian preconceptions about the noble savage from the eighteenth century is "an

---

[21] D. H. Lawrence, Robert Graves, Dorothy Edwards, Edwin Muir, Roy Campbell, *Scrutinies,* ed. Edgell Rickword (London: Wishart, 1928).

[22] Roy Campbell, "Wyndham Lewis: An Essay" (1931), in *Blast 3* (Santa Barbara, Cal.: Black Sparrow Press, 1984), p. 20.

entirely despicable and crass form of sentimentality."[23]

The 1918 novel *Tarr,* in which Lewis satirizes Parisian bohemia, is described by Campbell as "prophetic and inspired."[24] Campbell characterized *The Art of Being Ruled* as:

> . . . a colossal work which focuses from an entirely new point of view the whole modern social world in a state of transition, and the whole history of the modern social revolution from the time of Rousseau. . . . the liberal-democratic European idea is doomed, for in its tendency towards petty franchises and nationalisms and in its superficial idea of "freedom," it is anarchistically hostile to the organization of the white race as a whole, and is one of the chief causes of the decline of European power.[25]

Campbell also takes up the theme of the nature of liberal-democracy and plutocracy in describing *Doom of Youth* where, as Campbell puts it, "it is 'big business' that rules the state":

> Instead of centralising itself in the state it rules the masses impersonally and indirectly through the Press, which for all the "freedom" and "independence" of the individual, democracy can turn him into cannon-fodder in two seconds. . . . Big business, of course, with the gradual unification of trusts and cartels, becomes more and more like a dictatorial government, as in the bolshevik state—but not being identified with the life of the state, it operates independently of the welfare of

[23] Campbell, "Wyndham Lewis," p. 27.
[24] Campbell, "Wyndham Lewis," p. 23.
[25] Campbell, "Wyndham Lewis," p. 23.

the state, and quite irresponsibly . . .[26]

As for Bloomsbury, *The Apes of God* "crashes finally and triumphantly through the barriers of modern social and literary shams."[27] Although the essay was not published during Campbell's lifetime, his defense of Lewis was still costly to Campbell's career.

BULWARK OF CHRISTENDOM

In 1933 the Campbells left Provence for Spain due to financial hardship, despite the success of Campbell's acclaimed volume of poems, *Adamastor*. This was the final work to be well-received by the Bloomsbury crowd, while *The Georgiad* was met by a "conspiracy of silence," as the *Times Literary Supplement* would recall in 1950.

The Campbells arrived in Barcelona, where a right-wing electoral victory resulted in strikes and violence by the anarchists and machine guns were much in evidence on the streets. However, the Campbells were greatly impressed by the traditional Catholic culture.

Campbell described himself for the first time as a "Catholic" in his 1933 autobiography *Broken Record,* attacking both English Protestantism as "a cowardly form of atheism" and the Freudianism that pervaded the Bloomsbury progressives. He contrasted this with the "traditional human values" that continued to form the basis of Spanish culture. *Broken Record* was a break with modernism, Campbell writing: "The modern healer, who has usually more interest in, and sympathy with, the disease than the patient, spreads about ten infections for every one he cures, and invents ten chemical poisons for every cure."[28]

---

[26] Campbell, "Wyndham Lewis," p. 25.

[27] Campbell, "Wyndham Lewis," p. 37.

[28] Roy Campbell, *Broken Record* (London: Boriswood, 1934),

Despite the reference to Catholicism, Campbell had not yet converted, but spiritual questions had long occupied him. An interest in Mithraism had emerged in Provence, where traces of the cult still remained. Mithraism was the religion most favored by the Roman legions. Its strong martial ethos, together with the mythos of the slaying of the bull,[29] appealed to Campbell.[30]

However, he had also been strongly impressed with the faith and traditionalism of the fishermen and farmers among whom he had been so popular in Provence. His *Mithraic Sonnets* are a reflection of Campbell's own spiritual odyssey, beginning with Mithras and ending with the triumph of Christ, a mixture of the two religions. The Mithraic conquering sun, *Sol Invictus,* the byword of the Roman legions, becomes transmogrified as the Sun of the Son of God, "the shining orb" reflecting as a mirrored shield the image of Christ.[31]

It is with these vague feelings towards Christianity and Catholic culture that the Campbells moved south to the rural village of Altea in 1934. Campbell continued to sing the praises of Catholicism in martial terms, of the solar Christ as the "Captain" winning the battle of faith. Spain breathed the martial Catholic tradition, and in *The Fight* Campbell writes of an aerial dogfight for his soul, his "red self" of atheism shot down by the "white self" of the Solar Christ, "the unknown pilot." At Altea, Campbell was again impressed with the "freshness, bravery, and reverence" of the people. In this atmosphere, Campbell's whole family—actually at the initiative of his wife—converted to Catholi-

---

p. 154.

[29] See M. J. Vermaseren, *Mithras, the Secret God* (London: Chatto and Windus, 1963).

[30] Pearce, *Bloomsbury and Beyond,* p. 158.

[31] Roy Campbell, *Mithraic Emblems* (London: Boriswood, 1936).

cism in 1935 and were received by the village priest Father Gregorio.[32]

Campbell's daughter Anna related many years later that for her father, Spain was the last country left in Europe that was still a pastoral society while much of the rest had become industrialized under the influence of Protestantism. Such was Campbell's aversion to machinery that he never used a typewriter or learned to drive.[33]

At this time Campbell wrote "Rust," the rust of time that brings ruin to the intentions of those who would industrialize and modernize:

> So there, and there it gnaws, the Rust,
> Shall grind their pylons into dust . . .

LACKEYS OF CAPITALISM

Campbell's political outlook becomes coherent with his religious conversion. An article published in 1935 in the South African magazine *The Critic* shows just how clear Campbell's knowledge of politics now was:

> The artist as romantic "rebel" is the tamest mule imaginable. He dates from the industrial era and has been politicized to play into the hands of the great syndicates and cartels. First by dogmatizing immorality, breaking up the "Family," that one definitive unit that has withstood the whole effort of centuries to enslave, dehumanize, and mechanize the individual, thereby cheapening and multiplying labour. It is the "Intellectual" which had been chiefly politicized into selling his fellow mates to capitalism, whether the capitalism be

---

[32] Pearce, *Bloomsbury and Beyond*, p. 164.

[33] Anna Campbell Lyle, *Son of Valour*, pp. 84–85, cited in Pearce, *Bloomsbury and Beyond*, p. 166.

> disguised as a vast inhuman state[34] or whether a gang of individuals. The last century has seen more class-wars, and wars between generations, than any other period. They have been deliberately fostered by capitalism, of which bolshevism is merely an anonymous form.[35] Divide and rule, said Cicero: encourage your slaves to quarrel and your authority will be supreme. A thousand artists and reformers with the highest ideals have leaped ignorantly and romantically into these rackets, and by means of causing hate between man and woman, father and son, class and class, white and black, almost irretrievably embroiled the human individual in profitless, exhausting struggles which leave him at the mercy of the unscrupulous few.[36]

In 1936, Campbell met British Fascist leader Sir Oswald Mosley at the suggestion of Wyndham Lewis.[37] Although Campbell declined to join Mosley as British Fascism's official poet, his poetry was to appear in Mosley's journals.[38]

---

[34] A reference to communism.

[35] Spengler made this observation of the "capitalistic" nature of socialist movements: "There is no proletarian, not even a Communist, movement that has not operated in the interest of money, in the directions indicated by money, and for the time permitted by money—and that, without the idealists amongst its leaders having the slightest suspicion of the fact." See Oswald Spengler, *The Decline of the West,* 2 vols., trans. Charles Francis Atkinson (London: George Allen and Unwin, 1971), vol. 2, p. 402.

[36] Roy Campbell, "Uys Krige: A Portrait," *The Critic: A South African Quarterly* (Cape Town), vol. 3, no. 2; reprinted in *Collected Works*, vol. 4, p. 268.

[37] Pearce, *Bloomsbury and Beyond,* p. 199.

[38] His tribute to the Alcazar, having been besieged by the Spanish Reds, appeared in Mosley's *British Union Quarterly* in

TOLEDO, THE SACRED CITY

The Campbells next moved to Toledo, which had been Spain's capital under Charles V during the Holy Roman Empire. The city was isolated and timeless, medieval, full of churches, monasteries, convents, and shrines. The old fortress, the Alcazar, destined to play a pivotal role in the defense of Christendom against Bolshevism, served as a military academy. The city was full of priests, nuns, monks, and soldiers, a combination of the religious, the military, and the traditional that prompted Campbell to call Toledo the "sacred city of the mind."

The Left-wing Popular Front's assumption to power resulted in the release of communist and anarchist revolutionaries from jail amidst increasing political violence in Madrid and Barcelona and street fighting between Left-wing and Right-wing factions.[39] Churches were now being desecrated and destroyed throughout Spain.[40] The violence reached Toledo, despite its Rightist majority, where priests and monks were attacked and a church set ablaze.[41]

The Campbells sheltered several Carmelite monks in their home.[42] Despite the danger, Campbell's retort later was: "Better a broken head than a broken spirit every time!"[43] Campbell, well known for his anti-Bolshevik views and for his faith, was indeed severely beaten by government "Red" guards and paraded through the streets to police headquarters.[44] His gypsy friend, with whom he was riding at the time of his capture, "Mosquito" Bargas, was

---

1936. See below.

[39] Alexander, *Roy Campbell,* p. 148.

[40] Alexander, *Roy Campbell,* p. 158.

[41] Alexander, *Roy Campbell,* p. 159.

[42] Alexander, *Roy Campbell,* p. 160.

[43] Campbell, *Light on a Dark Horse,* p. 339.

[44] Alexander, *Roy Campbell,* p. 160.

murdered at the time of the arrest.[45] In his tribute to his friend, "In Memoriam of 'Mosquito,'" Campbell writes with typical stoicism and faith when beaten bloody and dragged through Toledo:

> I never felt such glory
> As handcuffs on my wrists.
> My body stunned and gory
> With toothmarks on my fists . . .

While Spain was on the verge of civil war and any display of faith was fraught with danger, the Campbells were confirmed into the Church by Cardinal Goma, Archbishop of Toledo and Primate of Spain, in a secret ceremony.

In July 1938, the government's Red guards killed parliamentary opposition leader Calvo Sotelo, the leader of the monarchists.[46] Four days later, the military under General Franco revolted against the government to restore order and liberty of worship. The Alcazar being a military academy, Toledo was easily taken by Nationalist troops, and peasants from the surrounding countryside fled to the city for refuge from their "proletarian liberators." The government militia from Madrid prepared to attack Toledo, and the Alcazar was bombed and shelled. The Campbells hid the rare and valuable archives of the Carmelite monks at their home for the duration of the Civil War, the Carmelite library having been razed.

Seventeen Carmelite monks were herded into the streets by the Red forces and shot. Among them was the Campbells' Father Confessor who died with a smile and the shout of "Long live Christ! Long live Spain!"[47]

---

[45] Pearce, *Bloomsbury and Beyond*, pp. 182–83.

[46] Pearce, *Bloomsbury and Beyond*, p. 184.

[47] Pearce, *Bloomsbury and Beyond*, p. 186.

In Campbell's excursion into the city he came across the Carmelites lying in the street and found the bodies of the Marist monks. Smeared in their blood on a wall was: "Thus strike the Cheka," a reference to the original Bolshevik secret police. In the city square religious artifacts from churches and private homes were tossed onto bonfires.

In the besieged Alcazar were 800 Civil Guards and 500 civilians, including over 200 children.[48] Under the command of Colonel Moscardó they held out, even as the Colonel's 24-year-old son Luis, captured by the Red forces, was compelled to telephone his father and say that he would be shot unless the Alcazar was surrendered. In an epic act of heroism and martyrdom that helped make the Alcazar a shrine to this day, the Colonel replied to his son: "Commend your soul to God, shout '*Viva España,*' and die like a patriot."[49]

Campbell's tribute to the Alcazar was published in Mosley's *British Union Quarterly*:

This Rock of Faith, the thunder-blasted—
Eternity will hear it rise.
With those who (Hell itself out-lasted)
Will lift it with them to the skies!
Till whispered through the depths of Hell
The censored Miracle be known . . .

The towers and trees were lifted hymns of praise,
The city was a prayer, the land a nun:
The noonday azure strumming all its rays
Sang that a famous battle had been won,
As singing his white Cross, the very Sun,

---

[48] Brian Crozier, *Franco: A Biographical History* (London: Eyre and Spottiswoode, 1967), p. 205.

[49] Crozier, *Franco,* p. 206.

The Solar Christ and the captain of my days
Zoomed to the zenith; and his will was done.[50]

The Campbells left Spain and returned to London. They felt isolated in England, where most of the literati supported the "Left" in the Spanish Civil War.[51] The family soon moved to a fishing village in Portugal, a nation that, under the corporatist regime of Salazar, retained the same spirit of faith and tradition as that for which Spain was fighting to restore.

Campbell returned to Spain as a correspondent for the British Catholic newspaper *The Tablet* and was given safe conduct to the Madrid front.[52] His desire to enlist in the Nationalist forces was frustrated, as the Nationalist authorities were insistent that he could do more good for the cause as a writer. Nonetheless, he was awarded the Cruz de San Fernando for saving life under fire, fourteen times.[53] With the conclusion of the Civil War, the Campbells reset-

---

50 Roy Campbell, "The Alcazar Mined," reprinted in *Selections from BUF Quarterly* (Marietta, Ga.: The Truth at Last, 1995), pp. 56–57.

51 When the *Left Review* surveyed 148 British writers as to whether they were "for, or against, the legal government and the People of Republican Spain . . . for or against, Franco and Fascism?" only five supported Franco. Fifteen including even Ezra Pound and T. S. Eliot, from whom one would expect a commitment to the Right, remained neutral. Shaw's answer was unclassified, and the rest were supportive of the Reds. Of course, the question was phrased in an absurd, loaded manner, but putting it differently would not likely have changed the results. See: Alastair Hamilton, *The Appeal of Fascism: A Study of Intellectuals and Fascism, 1919–1945* (New York: Macmillan, 1971), p. 259.

52 Pearce, *Bloomsbury and Beyond*, p. 206.

53 Campbell in a letter to Harvey Brit, 1956, cited by Pearce, *Bloomsbury and Beyond*, p. 326.

tled in Spain, and he was present at the Nationalist victory parade in Madrid.[54]

The Civil War resulted in the murder of 12 bishops, 4,184 priests, 2,365 monks, and around 300 nuns. George Orwell, who had gone to Spain along with others of the literati to fight with the Reds, was to remark that, "Churches were pillaged everywhere as a matter of course. In six months in Spain, I only saw two undamaged churches."[55]

FLOWERING RIFLE

Campbell's epic poem *Flowering Rifle*[56] is a detailed explanation of his political credo inspired by the Civil War. It is a tribute to his Catholicism and to Spain's faith and martyrdom, as well as a condemnation of the British intelligentsia. In his introductory note, Campbell explains that a hypocritical "humanitarianism" is the "ruling passion" of the British intelligentsia, which "sides *automatically* with the Dog against the Man, the Jew against the Christian, the black against the white, the servant against the master, the criminal against the judge."

As a form of "moral perversion" it was natural that such "humanitarians" sided with Bolshevik mass murderers. The poem begins with a description of the (fascist) salute, the "opening palm, of victory" the sign, of "palms triumphant foresting the day." By contrast is the clenched fist of communism, "a Life-constricting tetanus of fingers," the sign of an "outworn age" under which "all must starve under the lowest Caste." The Bloomsbury intelligentsia represents the connection between capitalism and communism.

---

[54] Pearce, *Bloomsbury and Beyond*, p. 224.

[55] George Orwell, *Homage to Catalonia*, vol. 6, *The Complete Works of George Orwell* (London: Secker and Warburg, 1980), p. 260.

[56] Roy Campbell, *Flowering Rifle* (London: Longman, 1939).

Behind these stand "the Yiddisher's convulsive gold": one of many allusions to the prominent role played by Jews in Communism and in the International Brigades.

Spain is heralded as a resurrected nation that might show the rest of Europe the path to regeneration and stand against Bolshevism "which no godless democracy could quell." The martyrs of the Nationalist cause are described in mystical terms, each death "a splinter of the Cross," each body building a cathedral to the sky. Nobility is achieved through suffering and sacrifice, as Christ, the "Captain" suffered. But when suffering and sacrifice are eliminated from life, mankind is "shunned by the angels as effete baboons."

José Antonio Primo de Rivera, the charismatic young leader of the Falangists, who had been shot without trial while in the custody of the Leftist government, was similarly eulogized:

Whose phoenix blood in generous libation
With fiery zest rejuvenates the nation . . .

The Marxist deaths, on the other hand, were vacuous, for their gods are economics, science, gold, and sex, and as exponents of abortion and birth control they are the essence of anti-life. But capitalism is just as much a debasement of man as communism:

To cheapen thus for slavery and hire
The racket of the Invert and the Jew
Which is through art and science to subdue.
Humiliate, and to pulp reduce
The Human Spirit for industrial use
Whether by Capital or by Communism
It's all the same despite their seeming schisms

Those who are debased the most are, under democracy,

elevated to positions of honor and state, elected by the voting masses who are mesmerized by the media and the literati, while the politicians hang about the League of Nations:

> That sheeny club of communists and masons
> He bombs the Arabs, when his Jews invade.

Britannia's trident had become a "graveyard spade" while condemning Germany and Italy. "Who from the dead have raised more vital forces . . ." Franco, Mussolini, and Portugal's Salazar had "muzzled up the soul destroying lie" of communism, and as Spain had shown, victory would come through nationhood, not League of Nations sanctions, wealth, or arms. Meanwhile, Britain shunned its unbought men, such as Campbell, who brings "the tidings that Democracy is dead."

When the Campbells travelled to Italy in 1938, the exiled Spanish King Alfonso XIII, who was greatly impressed with *Flowering Rifle*, cordially greeted them.[57] Of course the British literati were outraged, and even some Catholics felt the poem lacked "charity," but it did have its enthusiasts, such as Arthur Bryant, who were willing to speak out, while predictably Stephen Spender, one of the most prominent of the literary Bolsheviki, despite his *secret* admiration of Campbell's *style*, was scathing.[58]

War Service

Campbell and his wife returned to Toledo in 1939. But there was now widespread famine. Mary opened a soup kitchen and refurbished the damaged chapel by selling all her jewelry. Both literally gave their clothes away to help

---

[57] Pearce, *Bloomsbury and Beyond*, p. 217.

[58] Pearce, *Bloomsbury and Beyond*, pp. 218–19.

the distressed inhabitants.[59]

As the World War approached, Campbell considered that there would be two great contending forces: Fascism and Communism. With the exception of what he considered to be a pagan orientation in Germany, the Fascist states were eminently Christian and allowed Christians the right to live, whereas Bolshevism simply killed and degraded everything, being the enemy of every form of religion.[60]

However, despite his antagonism to the English bourgeoisie and democratic Britain, Campbell always had an admiration for the heroic spirit of the British Empire and a feeling for those Britons facing an enemy. He sought to enlist, although under no illusions about the justice of the Allied cause. His animosity by this time was against all systems, fascism, democracy, and bolshevism, which he dubbed as *Fascidemoshevism*.[61] The Hitler-Stalin Pact prompted Campbell's reassessment,[62] which is not to say that he ever considered rejecting his Rightist, Catholic beliefs.

His ideal was not the cumbersome state of any of these systems but that of small, self-reliant, and cooperative family based communities, like those he had experienced in Provence, Spain, and Portugal.

In the "Moon of Short Rations," Campbell considered the Allied cause to be that of both socialism and the multinational corporations, twin figures of a universal sameness. He saw that the post-war world would be ever more depersonalized and mechanical. Campbell could not sit still or take a soft option as a number of his pro-war Left-wing

---

59 Alexander, *Roy Campbell*, p. 182.

60 Pearce, *Bloomsbury and Beyond*, p. 225, citing a letter from Campbell to his mother, June 3, 1939.

61 Pearce, *Bloomsbury and Beyond*, p. 254.

62 Pearce, *Bloomsbury and Beyond*, p. 225.

intellectual accusers were doing while Britons marched to war. He lampooned these hypocrites such as Stephen Spender and Cecil Day-Lewis who had jobs at the Ministry of Information, when they attacked his "fascism," and he wrote "The Volunteer's Reply to the Poet" stating:

> Oh yes! It will be the same, but a bloody sight worse . . .
> Since you have a hand in the game . . .
> You coin us the catchwords and phrases
> For which to be slaughtered . . .

However, because of his age and a bad hip Campbell had to be content with the Home Guard until 1942, when he was recruited into the Army Intelligence Corps due to his skills in languages. Britain in wartime had in Campbell's view awakened from its "drabness" to become again a "warrior nation." Campbell was popular with the troops as a "grandfatherly" figure, and was stationed in East Africa. Suffering from malaria and a deteriorating hip condition that necessitated the use of a cane, he was discharged with an "excellent military record."

The Post-War World

The England of the post-war years returned to its drab routine and, worse still for Campbell, the prospects of an all-embracing welfare state. Campbell soon went back into fighting mode against the Left-wing poets, writing *Talking Bronco.*[63] Even Vita Sackville-West, part of the Bloomsbury clique, acclaimed this volume, calling Campbell "one of our most considerable living poets." Desmond MacCarthy, writing in the *Sunday Times,* regarded Campbell as "the most democratic poet," not politically, but in his feeling for the common man and for the common soldier. Others were

---

[63] The name that Stephen Spender had applied to Campbell.

of course outraged. Cecil Day-Lewis, another of the literary Bolsheviki, believed Campbell should be sacked as a "fascist" from the job he now had as producer of the BBC talk programs, since he was not fit to "direct any civilized form of cultural expression."[64]

Campbell was horrified by the Allied victory that had placed half of Europe under the USSR. For Campbell, the Cold War was a contention between two equally internationalist forces.[65]

His daughter Anna wrote in 1999 that Campbell admired all types of ethnic civilization as opposed to the mass conformity of Marxism and the globalization of the likes of McDonald's and Coca-Cola. His concern was in the nightmare of "everything becoming the same." He would have been "horrified by what the world has become now," she wrote.[66]

Despite Campbell's sensitivity to being called a "fascist," he was unapologetically a man of the "Right," of tradition and nationalism, and continued to forthrightly expound this position after the war in his poetry and essays. Writing in a Jesuit journal, he refers to the "Gadarene stampede" of progress for the want of two sensible standbys (a brake and a steering wheel). In "Tradition and Reaction," he writes: "A body without reactions is a corpse. So is a Society without Tradition."[67]

In 1949 Campbell left his job with the BBC to take over the editorship of *The Catacomb,* founded by his close friend,

---

[64] Cecil Day-Lewis to Stephen Spender, quoted in Pearce, *Bloomsbury and Beyond,* p. 271.

[65] Pearce, *Bloomsbury and Beyond,* p. 282.

[66] Anna Campbell Lyle to Joseph Pearce, June 9, 1999, quoted in Pearce, *Bloomsbury and Beyond,* p. 281.

[67] Roy Campbell, "A Decade in Retrospect," *The Month,* May 1950.

the poet Rob Lyle, as a defense of Catholic and Classical traditions against socialism and secularism. *The Catacomb* stopped publication in 1951.

In 1952, the family moved to Portugal, which had remained a bastion of Catholic civilization under Salazar. Before leaving England, Campbell got together with a number of South African literary friends, including Alan Paton and Laurens van der Post, and signed an open letter to the South African government protesting voting restrictions on the colored population.[68] However, Campbell's misgivings about the South African situation were not prompted by the liberal desire for a democratic, monocultural state. He feared that antagonism between the races would result in Bolshevism and the destruction of his rustic ideal. With the advent of black rule, free market capitalism was ushered in on the wings of Marxism and revolution, which would hardly have surprised Campbell. Today the ANC today calls globalization and trade liberalization the "correct path to Marxism-Leninism."[69]

In 1954, he gave his views on his native land while accepting an honorary doctorate from Natal University. In an off-the-cuff speech, much to the embarrassment of the liberal audience, he defended South Africa against England's condemnation of apartheid, ridiculing Churchill and Roosevelt, who had sold "two hundred million natives of Europe" to the far worse slavery of Bolshevism.[70]

While in the US on a speaking tour, he praised "the two greatest Yanks," Senator McCarthy and General MacArthur.[71]

---

[68] Alexander, *Roy Campbell*, p. 224.

[69] K. R. Bolton, "Multiculturalism as a Process of Globalization," *Ab Aeterno*, no. 1, November 2009, p. 27.

[70] Pearce, *Bloomsbury and Beyond*, pp. 318–19.

[71] Pearce, *Bloomsbury and Beyond*, p. 316.

On April 23, 1957, Campbell and his wife had a motor accident while returning from Spain to Portugal. Campbell's neck was broken, and he died at the scene. Mary survived him by 22 years.

Edith Sitwell, who converted to Catholicism through the example of the Campbells, remarked that he was, "The true Knight of Our Lady. . . . He died as he had lived, like a flash of lightning."[72]

Campbell, despite his rejection of affiliation with the pre-war British Union, remained a hero of the Right and was eulogized in Mosley's journal, *The European,* by Richard Aldington[73] and by Henry Williamson, who concluded by describing Campbell as "the only unencumbered man of genius I have known . . ."[74]

---

72 Edith Sitwell, *Taken Care Of* (New York: Atheneum, 1964), p. 166.

73 Richard Aldington, *The European,* vol. 12, no. 5, January 1959.

74 Henry Williamson, "Roy Campbell: A Portrait," *The European,* vol. 12, no. 6, February 1959, p. 358.

INDEX

Numbers in bold indicate a chapter or section of a chapter devoted to a particular topic.

About the Author

Kerry Bolton holds Doctorates in Theology and a Ph.D. h.c. He is a contributing writer for *Foreign Policy Journal* and a Fellow of the Academy of Social and Political Research in Greece. His books include *Revolution from Above* (London: Arktos Media, 2011). His articles have been published by both scholarly and popular media, including the *International Journal of Social Economics; Journal of Social, Political, and Economic Studies; Geopolitika; World Affairs; India Quarterly; The Occidental Quarterly; North American New Right;* Radio Free Asia; *Irish Journal of Gothic & Horror Studies,* Trinity College; *International Journal of Russian Studies,* and many others. His writings have been translated into French, German, Russian, Italian, Czech, Latvian, Farsi, and Vietnamese.

www.ingramcontent.com/pod-product-compliance
Lightning Source LLC
LaVergne TN
LVHW090939080826
845145LV00003B/806

* 9 7 8 1 9 3 5 9 6 5 1 4 5 *